CU00383733

THE DHARMA
OF CAPITALISM

NITESH GOR

THE DHARMA

OF CAPITALISM

A guide to mindful decision making in the business of life

KoganPage

LONDON PHILADELPHIA NEW DELHI

www.DharmaOfCapitalism.com
Nitesh.Gor@DharmaOfCapitalism.com

First published in 2010 in the United States by Platform Press, the nonfiction imprint
of Winans Kuenstler Publishing, LLC Doylestown, Pennsylvania 18901 USA
www.wkpublishing.com
Platform Press and colophon are registered trademarks

Publisher's note
Every possible effort has been made to ensure that the information contained
in this book is accurate at the time of going to press, and the publishers and
authors cannot accept responsibility for any errors or omissions, however
caused. No responsibility for loss or damage occasioned to any person acting, or refraining from action, as a result of the material in this publication
can be accepted by the editor, the publisher or the author.

First published in Great Britain in 2012 by Kogan Page Limited

Kogan Page Limited
120 Pentonville Road
London N1 9JN
United Kingdom
www.koganpage.com

© Nitesh Gor, 2012

British Library Cataloguing in Publication Data

A CIP record for this book is available from the British Library.

ISBN   978 0 7494 6422 6
E-ISBN 978 0 7494 6423 3

Typeset by Graphicraft Ltd, Hong Kong
Printed and bound in India by Replika Press Pvt Ltd

Dedicated to my grandfather who, whilst walking the path of Goodness, first showed me the way of Dharma.

CONTENTS

About the author   x
Acknowledgements   xi

Introduction   1

PART ONE
THE DHARMA IMPERATIVE   7

Social Responsibility 2.0   9
Capitalism's Higher Purpose   13
Decoding Dharma   15
The Dharma Stock Index   21
West Meets East   23

PART TWO
THE DHARMA TOOLBOX   27

The Dharma Diagnosis   29
The Three Modes   31
Dharma in Practice   35
Downstream Dharma   37
Goodness and Conscience   40
A Sample Dharmic Dilemma   44

PART THREE
THE DHARMA USER'S GUIDE   47

The Ignorance of the Lambs   49
Pharma Dharma: Wages of Ignorance   53
The Passion of the Capitalist   56
Dharma Drama: AOL Time Warner   59
Dharma Goodness: The Patience Payoff   62
Dharma Exposed: A Kodak Moment   66
The Three Modes, in Mind and Motion   68
Dharma Mumbo Jumbo   70

PART FOUR
DHARMA IN ACTION   73

Purpose-Driven Dharma   75
The Four Pillars of Goodness   77
Dharma Versus Dharma   79
Invisible Dharma   82
Know Your Mode   84
The Dharma of Human Resources   90
Getting The Dharma Boot   92
Dharm-anthropy   94

PART FIVE
THE DHARMA OF LEADERSHIP   103

The Pull of Dharma   105
Delegating Dharma   108
Corporate Dharma   117
Dharma Field Report   118
Dharmic Reset   120

Goodness Is In The Details   123
Leading In Style   125
The Five Roles of Successful CEOs   127
Accidental Leaders   129
You Are Here   130
Take The Best, Leave The Rest   131

ABOUT THE AUTHOR

NITESH GOR has served in executive, leadership and consulting roles in asset management, investment banking and the natural resource exploration industry. As co-founder and CEO of Dharma Investments, he oversaw development of the Dharma Indexes, introduced under licence by Dow Jones.

He holds an MBA from London Business School and a BA from the University of London.

Gor is chair of the I-Foundation, a charity establishing the first state-funded schools in the United Kingdom based upon dharma principles. Gor is also a regular columnist for *Forbes*.

He lives in London with his family.

ACKNOWLEDGEMENTS

I am indebted to my mentors whose personal examples led to the inspiration for this book, and from whom I have learnt so much about Goodness in the real world. I also wish to acknowledge:

* Foster Winans of Platform Press for understanding so well the subject matter and expertly and sensitively editing, consolidating, and restructuring the text;

* The many leaders and managers around the world who have allowed me to enter their organizations and homes to better understand the application of dharma and the Mode of Goodness;

* The folks at Letchmore Heath who, through their struggle for human rights, first engaged me in my own search for dharma;

* Prashun Popat, for his unfailing encouragement and guidance;

* Clifford de Souza, whose brainchild was the Dow Jones Dharma Index;

* Martin Fleming for his personal time spent helping refine many of my concepts and thoughts;

* Vandna Synghal for helping develop the first drafts of the manuscript;

* Rajesh Hirani of Filmwork Studios for the video shoots;

* Ajay Chag for portrait photography;

* Pradip Gajjar, Eddie Anobah, Kap Monet, Jay Shetty, Rishi and Sonal Singh, Dr Chetna Kang, Kirit Patel, Yuvraj Rana and Vijay Hirani for their feedback;

* My parents, wife, and two children, who tolerate my daily detours through Passion and Ignorance.

The best course is to satisfy one's
own conscience and leave
the world to form its own judgement.

MOHANDAS K. GANDHI

INTRODUCTION

When the student is ready,

the teacher will appear.

◉

BUDDHIST PROVERB

My interest in the relationship between money and ethics began at age seven, on a family journey from our home in London – where I'd spent most of my childhood – to the land of my birth, India. The trip was a pilgrimage for my devout Hindu parents, to visit holy sites and renew family ties.

On the long train ride between Mumbai and Goa, a ragged beggar entered the carriage in which we were riding and walked swaying down the aisle toward our seats, hand out, beseeching passengers in a raspy, mournful voice. Everyone ignored him. My heart ached with sympathy as he lurched by, empty palm extended in supplication. Even my parents looked away.

Soon another beggar appeared. I asked my father for change. He sighed, dug into his pocket, and produced a small coin that I dropped into the man's grimy hand as he passed. I settled back into the seat, feeling munificent.

Then a whole family of beggars appeared in the carriage doorway – a woman, a man with part of an arm missing, and a little girl with a dirty face, stained dress and bare, scuffed feet. The child, not much younger than I, led the adults down the aisle. She scanned the impassive faces with sad, pleading eyes and tiny outstretched hand. I gave my father's sleeve an urgent tug. He hesitated, then reached into his pocket. As he handed me a coin he said, 'That's it! No more after this.'

I was surprised. My father was my role model in matters of ethics and charity. He was kind and always going out of his way to help others back home. How could he refuse to help these terribly needy Indians with a few small coins?

He patted me on the knee. 'When we get to the next station, you'll understand.'

As the train jolted to a halt in the next city, he pointed out the window at the crowded platform. 'See all the beggars leaving the train? See what they are doing? They are all going over to that man standing by the wall. He is the boss of the beggars.'

The man my father identified was tidy, his clothes clean, leather shoes on his feet. The ragged beggars were walking up to him, handing him money, and pausing while he counted the coins and dropped them into a purse.

'That money you gave those people? They must turn it over to him. He lets them keep just enough for a bit of food. He decides who can beg on the trains and who cannot.'

I stared out the window, grappling with this revelation, as my father went on to explain that sometimes the overseers of the beggars deliberately disfigured them, to make them more pitiful so they would bring in more money. They might put out a child's eyes, or hack off a man's hand.

'So you see, giving them money actually hurts them more than it helps.'

My throat swelled. How was it possible to do the right thing but produce such a cruel result?

The incident was so disturbing that it stayed with me, in every detail, as I grew up. It was the starting point of a quest that, a quarter of a century later, led to the conclusion that doing good and living an ethical life means more than being generous, living green, following the Golden Rule, obeying the law and so on. It is so complex and nuanced that we need to find a simpler and more effective way of thinking and talking about it.

My humble contribution to that cause is the Dharma of Capitalism, which grew out of my role in developing the

Dharma Stock Index, tracking share prices of some 3,000 companies from around the globe that meet an extensive set of rigorous ethical standards.

Because it is so difficult to define 'doing the right thing', especially across the world's diverse cultures, you will find no new rules of behaviour here. Instead I hope to provoke readers into rethinking the process by which they make choices in business and in life by reinterpreting some ancient moral concepts that boil down to a simple but profound truth: better outcomes result from asking the right questions than from having the right answers.

What I came to understand during the years I mulled over my childhood experience was that every choice we make has a motive and an outcome and that the two are often at odds. Understanding our true motivations and taking responsibility for outcomes is at the core of the Dharma of Capitalism. Confronted with those beggars, I was motivated by the passion of the moment – I felt pity and guilt. I wanted to appear charitable. And I was oblivious of the outcome.

When adults allow their choices to be driven by passion, and when they ignore or fail to investigate outcomes, the result is too often flawed or unintended. We have many dramatic examples from which to choose.

Executives at Lehman Brothers, the once legendary but now defunct Wall Street investment house, knew the real estate mortgages they were buying, bundling and reselling a few years ago had been granted to unqualified buyers who were at high risk of defaulting. Blinded by large commissions and quick profits, these bankers chose to see, hear and speak no evil. The result was the overnight destruction of what had been one of the oldest and most-respected financial institutions in modern history, the unemployment of thousands, and the destruction of billions of dollars of wealth that had taken a century or more to create.

The failure to examine our motivations and own outcomes affects our lives in countless ways large and small. Whether you read it in one sitting, or randomly dip into chapters, my hope is that you will want to keep this book close by and refer to it when facing complex or important decisions.

If nothing else, the act of pausing to contemplate decisions before you make them will infuse your work and your life with greater intention and purpose.

WHAT IS DHARMA?

In Buddhist culture, dharma describes the moral and religious precepts set down 500 years BCE (before common era) by Buddha, a Nepalese-born teacher and philosopher. In Hindu culture, dharma refers to the search for life's universal truth and higher purpose.

The Dharma of Capitalism blends Hindu and Buddhist traditions with our current way of life. As used here,

the universal truth is that all people and cultures are connected by money and commerce and that there is a higher
purpose to economic activity than the short-term goals of
profit, wealth creation, and personal gratification.

Dharma is often confused or conflated with Karma, a
related concept in Hindu and Buddhist belief systems.
Karma describes the good or bad quality in every act or
deed as defined by the consequences, unseen as well as
seen. Karma might be thought of as life's running subtotal
of actions and outcomes, and dharma explains why it
matters.

PART ONE

THE DHARMA

IMPERATIVE

When I do good, I feel good;

when I do bad, I feel bad;

and that's my religion.

●

ABRAHAM LINCOLN

SOCIAL RESPONSIBILITY 2.0

The responsibility of a business is to 'increase its profits so long as it stays within the rules of the game'. It's been four decades since Milton Friedman, 1976 Nobel Laureate and the most influential economist of his time, made that declaration. In so doing he helped launch a free-market movement that ultimately ran amok, as illustrated in Oliver Stone's 1988 classic film, the era-defining *Wall Street* with its ironic battle cry of 'Greed is good!'

Twenty years later we reaped the bitter harvest of that movement – a global credit crisis, deep recession and insolvent governments, all traceable to a business and political culture that for three decades confused short-term profits and excess wealth with the higher purpose of life. Selfishness as the basis for happiness has been debunked and the soul of capitalism is in the process of being redefined.

The Art of War, the ancient Chinese text on battlefield strategy that every ambitious MBA was supposed to have read, is out. *The Bhagavad Gita*, the ancient Hindu scripture on battlefield morality, is in.

Nearly all of the developed world seems to be preoccupied with responsibility and sustainability – the green revolution, corporate reform, ethical behaviour, global thinking, local action. People, nations and businesses feel the pressure and the imperative to 'do the right thing'.

But what constitutes 'doing the right thing'? Does it mean reducing your carbon footprint? Does it mean following fair labour practices? Does it mean strong corporate governance? Does it mean giving more to charity? It is all these and much more.

Most of us know what we mean by doing the right thing, but we rarely think about it as a decision-making process. In our frantic world full of distractions, we tend to make choices on the fly in response to an expediency, crisis or opportunity. We rarely have or take the time to think through our choices, acting instead on instinct or intuition and hoping for the best.

In business, where decision-making is already a process, it's mostly about numbers – metrics – and about keeping your nose clean and your head down. Half of the more than 200 CFOs (chief financial officers) and investment professionals polled in a 2008 survey by consulting giant McKinsey & Co. said corporate social responsibility (CSR) is first a compliance issue – a headache and a threat – before it is a positive force for change.

It's no surprise that many companies focus their CSR energies opportunistically, without a unifying philosophy. Ask Campbell Soup executives about the company's CSR programme and you may learn that they've reduced annual consumption of packaging materials by hundreds of tons or that their packing processes have been redesigned to save thousands of gallons of fresh water.

Businesses are managed by the numbers, which explains why executives tend to adopt methods of demonstrating corporate responsibility that are easiest to measure. 'If you cannot tie your efforts directly to the business', a Campbell executive once acknowledged, 'you lose support'.

The Dharma of Capitalism recognizes that prejudice and politics play a role in business decisions, but going green, sponsoring an inner-city mentoring programme, or participating in any number of other beneficial programmes or practices do not by themselves constitute the higher purpose. Without a philosophy and committed leadership, these activities are reduced to ticks on a to-do list.

One of the challenges in coming up with a core set of principles and a decision-making process for doing the right thing is that there are a growing and possibly infinite number of definitions. The movement towards compassionate commerce and individual integrity has been a global social revolution bubbling up from below in thousands of places in thousands of forms.

On the macro scale, business leaders like Warren Buffett and Bill Gates have established enormous foundations to support the development of better health care among the world's poorest peoples. The Sea Shepherd Conservation Society – a radical breakaway group from Greenpeace – has engaged in commercial sabotage and dangerous high-seas confrontations to thwart Japanese whalers.

On the micro level, billions of individual decisions are made all day, every day, that may not hasten a disease cure or save the life of an endangered creature, but that do have outcomes. In a shrinking, crowded world where individual action may seem insignificant and consequences are often out of sight and mind, what should be the standard for 'the right thing'? How can we tell if we're doing it?

The boundaries on our diverse, economically vibrant planet are fading. For the same reason we have to write new legal codes to govern international transactions, we need a common moral code that transcends belief systems and cultural differences. Why we need it is made clear every day in the news:

A decision to cut corners in a processing plant in a remote Asian village produces an outcome in Chicago when contaminated pet food kills the beloved family cat.

The decision by a Western recycling company to ship millions of old computers overseas turns a Chinese village into a toxic wasteland where peasants toil over crude coal stoves inhaling carcinogenic fumes from the heavy metals they're melting off circuit boards.

Pirated software brings prosperity to an impoverished town, but a hemisphere away it renders an innovative technology company so unprofitable it must close its doors and put its employees on the street.

Decisions by Wall Street investment bankers lead to a global credit crisis that causes economic dislocation from the alleys of Dublin to the souks of Dubai.

In this seamless world, we need a practical and universal framework for evaluating business and life decisions across borders and cultures to increase the chances that good intentions yield good results. The future of humankind may one day hang in the balance.

CAPITALISM'S HIGHER PURPOSE

The Dharma of Capitalism – the higher purpose of for-profit economic activity – begins with ancient concepts expressed in Hinduism and Buddhism, two philosophies that share with later faiths high aspirations for human behaviour. Virtually every society has a similar value at the core of its code of acceptable conduct: the Golden Rule is as old as Confucius and a central tenet in one form or another of all major faiths.

We know that bad choices result from motivations such as greed and fear and from willing or wilful ignorance: 'It's not my problem.' 'As long as you make your numbers, I don't care how you did it.' 'What they don't know won't hurt them.'

The dharmic concept of higher purpose transcends religion and goes beyond the aspiration for people and institutions to act charitably or altruistically. Dharma is a philosophy that describes a way of looking at every decision from both ends – what are our real motivations, and are we conscious and caring about the outcomes, as opposed to the output?

For example, the Dharma of Capitalism would suggest that giving money to Indian railway beggars out of guilt and a desire to impress an elder is a tainted motive, driven by shame and pride while being oblivious to the consequences. A mortgage broker who pays for his child's college tuition through commissions earned by selling mortgages to unqualified home buyers is motivated by expediency, choosing to ignore or trivialize the likely outcome of bankruptcy, foreclosure, eviction and attendant suffering.

Why does it matter? Yes, those coins in the little girl's hands will end up in the purse of a mobster, but she will at least get something to eat. Yes, the home-buyer may have bitten off more than he can chew, but it's his decision and who can say how it will turn out? The broker wants to give his child the best education he can manage, so he justifies his actions as serving a good cause.

What's the harm? The answer is often unclear in the moment and only becomes obvious when it's too late.

Giving money that ends up supporting a brutal crime syndicate degrades a culture, contributes to more criminal activity, weakens the social fabric, and makes life more difficult and dangerous for everyone. Mortgage brokers who exploited easy credit and lax oversight to encourage people to buy unaffordable houses subsequently found themselves facing lawsuits, unemployment, stained résumés and the enmity of communities ravaged by foreclosures.

The Dharma of Capitalism is based on the premise that doing the right thing is more than a noble idea or a compliance issue – it's practical and it's profitable. In the day-to-day decisions we make in life and business it's much more complicated, which sparked this effort to bring some structure to the process.

DECODING DHARMA

The Indian beggar episode taught me a lesson about consequences. From his deathbed, my grandfather taught me a lesson about personal responsibility. He was 75 years old, living with our family in London, when he fell and suffered a hip fracture that kept him confined to the house. His health steadily declined over several months.

One day he summoned the family and issued instructions for tidying up the loose threads of his affairs. He assigned a neighbour the task of going to the local greengrocer to pay off his outstanding balance – about just over two pounds, less than four US dollars.

Our neighbour assured him he would take care of it the next day, but my grandfather was adamant. 'It must be done today.' The neighbour did as he was asked and brought back the receipt. That night, my grandfather died. Balancing the books of his life seemed to have cleared his conscience, allowing him to cross the threshold in peace.

The sudden urge of the gravely ill to settle accounts – both financial and emotional – is a common instinct. We spend entire lifetimes communicating, but the most important words a person utters or writes often come at the end.

My grandfather died when I was old enough to understand what was happening and young enough to be awestruck by the drama and its impact on our family. He had summoned his last ounce of strength to focus on a matter anyone else would have considered insignificant under the circumstances, but for him was an important part of following his dharma. It was a defining moment for all of us, profoundly so for me.

This lesson in ethics sparked an avocation that included studying the belief system, Hinduism, into which I had been born. Growing up all but one year of my life within commuter distance of the two most important cities in the West – London and New York – I was always conscious of my cultural otherness. I began reading about all religions with particular interest in what they had to say about doing the right thing.

While morality dealt with the right course of action, ethics was concerned with character. One could be moral and do the right thing, yet be a person of poor character and ethically lacking. It became clear that a new construct was needed that combined character and motive – ethics – with right action – morality.

Aside from my family heritage, Hinduism and Buddhism appealed to me because, unlike other faiths, the dharmic ethical code encourages doing the right thing with a carrot instead of a stick. Rather than invoking shame and punishment for violating rules and commandments, the ancient scriptures speak of our worst instincts not as sins but as natural tendencies to be acknowledged and tamed in the service of wise, compassionate thinking and behaviour. Rather than the concept of evil, the scriptures speak of the struggle to consistently be good.

An individual's dharma, or moral imperative, is said to evolve (or devolve, in the case of criminals and other corrupt or immoral people) as he or she journeys through life. As a result, if you asked a million Indians to define dharma you might well get a million different answers. The common usage implies righteousness, rightful or cor-rect action, behaviour codes, ethics and so on. Otherwise, dharma is a fluid concept, dependent on context.

There is material dharma as opposed to spiritual dharma. There are different dharmic expectations depending on whether one is young, single, married, older and so on. All these different dharmas share a common purpose – to help people remain mindful of the motivations and consequences of every decision they make, no matter how minor.

In the years following my grandfather's death, my interest in studying dharmic ideas about justice, wisdom and ethics continued to blossom. For a time I thought I wanted to become a physician. I got as far as the first year of medical school before being distracted by something I found more interesting. The Hindu community in suburban London was waging a campaign to preserve and support a local theological college and place of worship in Letchmore Heath, a small village of about a hundred homes.

It was a cause I'd first become involved with when I was 17, after returning to the UK from three years living and attending school in the New York suburbs. The local authorities wanted to close the institution. The number of visitors had grown so much that the once-quiet temple was now a busy venue. The added traffic on the village streets had become a nuisance. Local council officials invoked the local planning laws to declare the building's use unauthorized.

By the shutdown deadline of March 1994, a group of activists including myself had organized one of the largest public protests London had ever seen. An estimated 36,000 people of many different faiths showed up in front of Parliament to support the cause.

Two more years of protest and activism finally won us permission to keep the temple in Letchmore Heath open. Several years later, as part of an affiliated charity, we won government funding to build Britain's first state-supported school based on dharmic principles. It was also cited as the most environmentally friendly school in the country.

The time spent on these campaigns made it impossible to keep up with my medical studies so I left and earned a pharmacy degree, only to discover during my internship that the work was uninspiring.

In 2001, in the trough of the post-dotcom bubble, some friends and I tried to launch a company to market business software services that were outsourced to India. Our timing was off and we failed to raise the necessary capital.

Along the way, I had become fluent in dharmic principles and realized that in order to put them into practice in a business setting I needed to know more about how business works. I returned to the classroom to earn an MBA from the London Business School.

My career finally began, as an intern for a business consultancy. The singular goal of the firm was to raise the value of client company shares, by almost any means necessary. When I saw an ethical problem or suggested we could help clients with philanthropic goals, I was told the firm's job did not include worrying about morality or charity. 'That's up to the shareholders.' It was a heartless, soulless sort of enterprise and within a year I had moved on.

This time I was careful to choose a consulting firm that exhibited a social conscience. I joined a group of ambitious men and women caught up in the management consultancy boom. Many of my colleagues shared my idealism and my interest in ethics and charitable works, but they thought the first step was to become wealthy. 'Then I can set up a foundation and really make a difference.'

That appears sound in principle, but in practice it rarely happens. For every Bill Gates, Warren Buffett and Richard Branson, there are millions for whom there will never be so much money that they can give it away. Also, the 'earn now, donate later' model suggests it might be all right to cut corners or make a compromise here and there to become wealthy, so long as one intends to use the money for good purposes.

In India, where bribery and tax evasion are so prevalent they are practically line items in cash-flow calculations, many wealthy Hindu business people who benefit by the system are also generous contributors to their temples. The outcome appears to be good, but the motivation is greed and the appearance of piety. The true outcome is starving public agencies of the money needed to deliver basic services.

At the new consulting firm, we young recruits were expected to channel our idealist enthusiasm into working impossibly long hours. We were encouraged to sacrifice our private lives to prove our passion to get ahead. The atmosphere was so competitive and unhealthy that one of the partners felt compelled to participate in a conference call from the hospital bed where, just two hours earlier, she had given birth. Once again, I cast around for something more suited to my own sense of higher purpose.

THE DHARMA STOCK INDEX

In my search for business people who were interested in socially responsible investing, a colleague suggested creating an investment vehicle based on dharmic principles.

During more than a year of research, in partnership with the Hindu Studies Centre at Oxford University, we brought together a panel of some two dozen experts in the fields of philosophy, religion, business practices and investments. The first step was to define the global universe of publicly traded shares from which we could pick – market capitalization of $500 million and above. Then we winnowed the pack down to about 3,000 stocks.

In 2008, Dow Jones & Co., publisher of the *Wall Street Journal* and licenser of a number of market indexes such as the Islamic-based Dow Jones Sharia Index, licensed the Dharma Index. The Index is intended to yield a market-competitive return (in line with general indexes such as the Standard & Poor's 500) on a basket of companies that meet the most rigorous standards for non-violence and for custodianship – a term that was once applied solely to shareholders but that today includes all stakeholders in any endeavour.

Out of some 15,000 candidate companies, finalists must pass muster in the areas of corporate governance, environment, ethics, product impact, labour conditions and human rights. Among the more obvious exclusions are alcohol, tobacco, defence, gambling, adult entertainment, meat products and industries that use animals for testing.

More detailed filters look at treatment of employees, work environment, corporate transparency and so on. The Dharma Index, for example, excludes certain soft drink makers because they also market alcoholic beverages.

On a superficial level, avoiding so-called sin and animal-exploitative industries can be seen as specific cultural or religious matters. Inversely, Western cultures acknowledge the negative social effects of addictive gambling and alcohol abuse but consider those industries legitimate and bankable. Meanwhile, vegetarianism in the West is almost a belief system by itself, driven by environmental, health-related or aesthetic concerns. For Hindus and Buddhists, the avoidance of gambling, alcohol and meat are ethical issues.

For the purposes of the Dharma Index, sin industries are excluded for the more profound reason that they cater to demonstrably self-destructive behaviour. Animal products and testing are excluded not only because of the violence and suffering, but also for the practical reason that meat production, for example, is an inefficient and unsustainable source of protein that also wreaks havoc on the environment. To produce 1,000 calories in edible flesh uses up the equivalent of more than 6,000 calories worth of edible soyabeans. Livestock production generates nearly a fifth of the world's greenhouse gases, more than transportation.

Just as there is an identifiable outcome that requires us to find a charitable alternative to giving coins to enslaved beggars, or a practical outcome that should make a mortgage broker feel a sense of custodianship about the risks to customers are being exposed, there are common sense reasons to avoid investing in companies whose activities make harmful outcomes possible. If you believe that harm to some of humanity is ultimately harm to all of humanity, it is in our own interests. In that sense, dharma is objective, non-religious and pragmatic.

WEST MEETS EAST

The Dharma of Capitalism aspires to merge the best characteristics of the ethical cultures of East and West. Each has much to offer the other.

For much of the twentieth century, the West exported to the rest of the world entrepreneurial energy and the tools to create prosperity and independence. Now the previously underdeveloped nations are catching up, and Eastern traditions and philosophies are rapidly informing the way we live and do business in the West.

Insurer Liberty Mutual ran a series of television ads in 2006 that expressed the concept of dharma without mentioning it. The ads, known as the 'do the right thing commercials', were a collection of snippets portraying strangers pausing in their busy days to help each other. Each person who was helped, in turn, helps another in an unbroken string of good deeds inspired by other good deeds, until the last person helped is the first person we saw helping. The ads portray the dharmic awareness of the interconnectedness of all things.

Corporate-sponsored meditation programmes to reduce stress are becoming accepted in the workplace at companies as small as a Swedish bus company and as large as sports-shoe marketer Reebok International.

'Karma Capitalism' is a term now being used in leading business schools such as Harvard, University of Pennsylvania and Dartmouth where students are reading *The Bhagavad Gita*, the ancient Hindu text about a warrior prince facing a moral dilemma.

By some estimates, one in ten professors in the top MBA programmes in the United States are of Indian heritage, raised with Hindu traditions. In 2010, Harvard University named Mumbia-born Nitin Nohria to become the tenth Dean of the Business School. Indian-born business consultants are playing a growing role in reshaping best practices in the West, teaching executives to take a more holistic approach that puts purpose before goals and stakeholders before stockholders.

Marquee business figures are publicly embracing Eastern philosophies, most notably Bill Gross, a familiar face to followers of business news as the head of Pacific Investment Management Co. (PIMCO), the world's largest bond mutual fund. Gross, whose first career was gambling, is now a self-professed Buddhist.

'Inclusive capitalism' is a new expression coined by the late C.K. Prahalad, a business consultant and University of Michigan professor ranked among the world's most influential business thinkers. He defined it as 'the idea that corporations can simultaneously create value and social justice'.

The goal of this book is to offer a decision-making framework for those who share that view and seek that outcome.

PART TWO

THE DHARMA

TOOLBOX

Think no vice so small that you may commit it, and no virtue so small that you may overlook it.

●

CONFUCIUS

THE DHARMA DIAGNOSIS

Doing the right thing all the time is nearly impossible. For starters, it is often difficult to feel confident about what is the right thing, especially as life becomes ever more complex and outcomes ever more numerous and public.

Then there is the problem of human nature. Moral relativism – the rationalization that our bad behaviour is less bad than that of others – is distressingly common. Furthermore, most of us have an instinctive need to conform even when doing so results in choices that go against what we know in our hearts is right.

A frequently cited example is the infamous 1971 Stanford University Prison Experiment which divided a group of students into prisoners and guards and then confined them to a makeshift prison environment to act out their assigned roles. In just a few days the guards became so sadistic and the prisoners so depressed that the experiment had to be cut short.

The study's architect, psychologist Philip Zimbardo, would later write about this phenomenon, which he called the Lucifer Effect: almost anyone, given the right situation and influences, can be made to abandon their scruples and cooperate in violence and oppression. The Stanford Prison Experiment is an extreme illustration of something that happens to people on a daily basis in every aspect of their lives. They choose the path of least resistance or give in to their preconceived ideas and prejudices.

This is a well-documented problem that often stems from what social scientists call confirmation bias – the tendency of humans to give greater weight to information that confirms what they already believe or have experienced. Confirmation bias is said to explain why people hold an investment even as its value plunges. Their biases block out bad news and only allow in that information that confirms the basis on which they made the investment.

Confirmation bias is a problem because it interferes with mindful decision-making. Emily Pronin, a Princeton University professor, ran an experiment in which she showed subjects one of two photos of a man she identified as an investment adviser, and asked them how much of a hypothetical $1,000 stake they would trust him to invest.

For one photo, her model wore a suit and tie. In the other, he dressed in khakis and a polo shirt. The man in the suit got an average of $535. The same man in casual clothing got only $352.

Pronin also conducted behavioural studies that documented yet another flaw embedded in human perception: people feel better when they can make quick decisions and move on as opposed to the more difficult task of exercising patience and taking time to contemplate. We seem to have a natural tendency towards lazy, uncritical thinking.

One of the most prevalent myths is that people with good material fortune are happier than the rest of us. Numerous studies have found that people who suffer a devastating loss or physical calamity are, over time, just as happy as people who win the lottery or experience some other dramatically positive event. It turns out that people who have the most choices available to them – such as the wealthy – are actually less happy than those whose choices are limited, even someone who becomes permanently confined to a wheelchair.

Harvard psychologist Daniel Gilbert has studied this counterintuitive behaviour and written about it in his book *Stumbling On Happiness*. 'When our ambition is unbounded', he says, 'it leads us to lie, to cheat, to steal, to hurt others, to sacrifice things of real value. When our fears are unbounded and overblown, we're reckless, and we're cowardly.'

THE THREE MODES

Hindu and Buddhist philosophies break down human behaviour into three basic instincts or tendencies: creation, preservation and destruction. These three gunas, as they are known by their Sanskrit name, describe a cycle of evolution that should sound familiar. In love, for example, relationships tend to begin with passion, evolve into commitment and marriage, and too often end in boredom or rancor.

In business, the cycle similarly begins with the passion required to invent things, innovate processes, and build companies. The second step is making those companies profitable, sustainable and responsible. Finally, when we aren't mindful, they become casualties of complacency and carelessness, as did Wall Street investment banks that bet heavily on risky credit vehicles.

The response to the destructive phase is often focused on blame, punishment and regulation aimed at keeping it from happening again. These are passionate reactions that assume we can engineer better outcomes by isolating bad people and discouraging bad behaviour.

But the history of business is built on failure. The nature of capitalism is a 'perennial gale of creative destruction', observed economist Joseph Schumpeter in 1942.

The Dharma of Capitalism explains the gunas as three principal motives or modes of behaviour by which every decision can be assessed – the Modes of Ignorance, Passion and Goodness. In ascending order, they also describe increasing levels of awareness. The process of good decision-making begins with evaluating the choices we face to determine whether the primary motivation is complacency, carelessness or oversight (ignorance); greed, pride or some short-term benefit or reaction (passion); or whether the motivation takes into account all stakeholders and the decision is informed by knowledge of and custodianship for outcomes (goodness).

The Three Modes are by definition hierarchical: from the inaction of Ignorance we move up the scale to the activity of Passion and from there strive to achieve the balance and mindfulness of choices made primarily in the Mode of Goodness. There is no finish line or mountain top in this process. All three of the Modes are at work in almost every situation and in every person, to one degree or another.

If you accept the dharmic notion that there is a higher purpose to business and money than profit and pleasure, the Modes will help you stay on track by identifying which is dominant at any given time:

* The Mode of Goodness: Often the tough choice, to act mindfully, with knowledge, purpose and a desire for the long-term benefit of all, characterized by fairness, transparency and trust. This is the mode in which we resist quick fixes and cutting corners, and consider the lasting and unseen consequences of every action and choice.

* The Mode of Passion: The alluring choice, acting on the desire for short-term pleasure or results, characterized by pride, narcissism, extremes, unpredictability. This is the engine of greed, addiction and risk-taking, but also of inspiration, innovation and entrepreneurial success.

GOODNESS

ENLIGHTENED
steeped in knowledge
balanced, regulated, enthusiastic
principled, selfless
Keyword: KNOWLEDGE

VALUES-BASED LEADER
noble, determined, courageous
learned, charitable
Keyword: RESPECT

AGGRESSIVE CONTROLLER
intense, active, proud, exploitative
greedy, erratic, capable, accomplished
Keyword: POWER

OPPORTUNIST
materialistic, hard working
short-term minded
Keyword: WEALTH

BLIND FOLLOWER
inclined to laziness, procrastination
dependent on others
susceptible to corruption
Keyword: CONFORMITY

PASSION

PASSION

IGNORANCE

* The Mode of Ignorance: The lazy choice, acting out of carelessness or disregard for consequences, characterized by lethargy, cynicism, a desire for quick relief from suffering, taking the easy way out.

The graphic representation that follows provides a shorthand visual of what's meant by the Modes, how they overlap and how they interact.

DHARMA IN PRACTICE

In consulting for business leaders and investors, the Three Modes helps me guide companies towards socially responsible and ethical choices.

In one instance, a start-up, high-tech company in the energy sector was in the final stages of securing major funding and the directors had to choose the corporation's official home. Their legal and tax experts had advised them to base the company in the Cayman Islands to take advantage of low tax rates. In my role as a consultant on strategic and ethical issues, I challenged the executives to look beyond the immediate benefit of having more cash to grow the business – the Mode of Passion.

Although greed is the wrong word for the desire to reduce costs, avoiding taxes is hardly the same as finding a cheaper source of raw materials or downsizing payroll. Dodging the taxman may be perfectly legal and may satisfy the aims of shareholders, but when evaluated through the lens of the Dharma of Capitalism, as a motivation it fails to acknowledge or take responsibility for the outcomes for diverse stakeholders. It is made in the Modes of Passion and Ignorance.

The directors expected the company to do most of its business and have its principal operations centre in the United States. I pointed out that by focusing solely on the short-term benefit, they were ignoring the impact the company's operations would have on local and national infrastructure. They would be getting a free or cheap ride for essential public services such as clean water, sewage, police and fire protection, as well as the robust national defence, judicial and political systems needed to provide a stable environment in which to attract investment capital and to operate.

My challenge to them: 'If you're going to depend on US services to run your company effectively, shouldn't you be paying for them?'

While domiciling in the Caymans might be profitable in the short run, I asked if they had considered what might happen if US authorities later decided to crack down on tax havens. One director replied, 'We can always relocate to another jurisdiction.' When I pointed out that this could cause quite an operational disruption, he suggested, 'We could choose a jurisdiction with limited ties to the US.'

Many businesses have legitimate reasons for choosing an offshore structure for some or all of their activities, but this was not such a case. The directors decided the stress of maintaining a questionable offshore presence was greater than the benefit. In the end the directors agreed with my analysis and registered the company in the United States. They said, 'At least we can sleep at night.'

DOWNSTREAM DHARMA

Ignorance and Passion are the troublesome Modes, but the terms are not meant to suggest value judgements nor are they evil forces. They are natural aspects of the human condition. By monitoring the role that passion and ignorance play in our motivations, we become more thoughtful and purposeful in our decision-making. We become motivated to act, and we give ourselves time to ponder implications of our actions before rushing into things.

Out of all this, we are more likely to do the right thing with greater consistency, especially if we apply this process of self-assessment to every aspect of life, no matter how mundane.

Decisions made in the Mode of Goodness are done with knowledge and deliberation. They are well thought out. The person operating in this mode typically follows a clear plan of action, hoping to achieve very specific goals and targets, all of which have been assessed for long-term gain and the repercussions on others.

The Mode of Goodness might be thought of as the downstream view. We know that dumping toxins in a stream contaminates water miles away, damages resources, and causes disease and economic loss. Every action produces a reaction – even the beating of a butterfly's wings is said to contribute to the weather half a world away. The Mode of Goodness aspires to just that level of awareness.

As an old English children's rhyme puts it:

> For *want of a nail the shoe was lost.*
> For *want of a shoe the horse was lost.*
> For *want of a horse the rider was lost.*
> For *want of a rider the battle was lost.*
> For *want of a battle the kingdom was lost.*
> All *for the want of a nail.*

Even when we set out to do good, even when we think we're being helpful, knowledge of the downstream effect matters. As I discovered about the beggars on the Indian trains, you can't assume you're doing the right thing just because it looks or feels that way.

On a much larger scale, a good example is what happened as a result of the explosion of micro-finance, a multibillion dollar global phenomenon that has attracted large private-equity and other investment pools. Well over $1 billion of capital has found its way to India where, like elsewhere, it was lent out in thousands of micro-loans of a few hundred dollars each. The borrowers were to use the money to start or grow micro-businesses, such as street stalls and workrooms.

Because the loans were so small, some Indian lenders doled them out with little or no investigation nor borrower support in the form of education and guidance. The default rate was predictably high. For these capital pools to earn investors a competitive return, the effective interest on the micro-loans exceeded 20 per cent, putting borrowers at a disadvantage from the start.

The bigger problem among these lenders was that borrowers, many of whom had never earned more than a few dollars a week and had never run a business, frequently spent some or all of the money on living expenses and luxuries. There was so much micro-finance money available from so many sources that people discovered they could borrow three or four times on the same promise.

A woman living in a shantytown who had taken out multiple loans and spent some of the money on a television, told a *Wall Street Journal* reporter that micro-finance 'increased our desire for things we didn't have'. Instead of opportunity, those micro-loans caused people like her to feel envy and greed; then when the day of reckoning arrived, regret and guilt.

Somewhere far upstream of that woman, who lost everything she owned and wound up poorer than she was before, were some socially responsible investors in another hemisphere who believed with all their hearts that they were doing the right thing. They thought they were acting in the Mode of Goodness, but the good was undone by ignorance – they had taken the outcome for granted.

In contrast, not-for-profit micro-lender Grameen Bank, based in Bangladesh, understood the culture and social dynamics of villages in its market and was able to manage its default rates to keep them low. The mixed history of micro-finance in India illustrates what happens when motivation and outcome are out of synch.

GOODNESS AND CONSCIENCE

Just as ignorance and passion are viewed through the dharmic lens as natural tendencies, goodness as used here does not imply a state of grace or exaltation. Someone who predominantly acts in the Mode of Goodness will simply experience happiness or a sense of accomplishment, along with insight and wisdom.

People who specialize in particular areas of research might fall into this category, especially when they are working for the benefit of others – a dedicated scientist hoping to remedy a disease to save lives, for example. He or she acts with the intensity and energy of someone in the Mode of Passion but is motivated by a greater good.

On the other hand, just as in the micro-finance example, it's possible to be a dedicated scientist while acting outside the Mode of Goodness. If the central motivation is personal gain involving the exploitation of others, the Mode of Passion is at work. If the scientist is unconcerned about the outcome, it's the Mode of Ignorance. Often, it is some combination of the two.

Thinking about motivations and caring about outcomes are the twin imperatives of the Dharma of Capitalism. They are the bookends of the process of determining the right thing to do.

No less an expert than Adam Smith, the Scottish moral philosopher who is considered to be the father of modern economics, expressed this concept in dharmic fashion in the eighteenth century. In his seminal work, *The Wealth of Nations*, Smith may have been the first to define the role of social responsibility in the modern pursuit of profit.

Smith wrote of 'the misery and disorders of human life [that] seems to arise from overrating' the accumulation of wealth and status. Of the benefits, he said,

> *None of them can deserve to be pursued with that passionate ardour which drives us to violate the rules either of prudence or of justice, or to corrupt the future tranquillity of our minds, either by shame from the remembrance of our own folly, or by remorse for the horror of our own injustice.*

Shame and guilt are among the most corrosive outcomes of decisions and actions dominated by ignorance and passion. Perhaps the most compelling argument for doing the right thing, for consciously acting in the Mode of Goodness, is that doing the wrong thing often leaves us with a chronic, low-grade fever of guilt. A burdened conscience can become a stubborn enemy.

We can talk our way through bad times and persuade ourselves it could always be worse, and we can rationalize a bad call to make the guilt easier to tuck away. But guilt and shame are relentless.

'There's no place that deception can stop', observed Conrad N. Hilton, founder of the Hilton Hotels empire. He said,

> It has to start with self-deception, even if it's only the self-deception of believing that we can get away with it. True, sometimes we are not 'discovered'. But all of modern psychology and psychiatry is based on the belief that our self-deceptions drive things into our subconscious where they make all kinds of trouble.

That seems to hold true for star athletes who feel compelled to confess to having taken performance-enhancing anabolic steroids. Two of the most-celebrated players in baseball history, Barry Bonds and Mark McGwire, both had their professional accomplishments stained by such revelations.

In McGwire's case, he also lied about it to a congressional subcommittee. In the Mode of Passion he abandoned the principles of his profession to get ahead. In the Mode of Ignorance, he was careless about potential outcomes including the enmity of his fans, potentially injuring his health, and a perjury conviction. Nearly ten years after the fact, the guilt (and suspicion) had become so bad he felt he had to come clean. Instead of a 'shoo-in' for the Baseball Hall of Fame, he will for ever be remembered as a cheater.

McGwire, Bonds and others like them are no more flawed than the rest of us. What makes them object lessons are the size and scope of their self-induced tragedies. They failed to answer the question we all should be asking ourselves: 'Are my motives good, have I considered all the possible outcomes, and am I doing something my conscience tells me I shouldn't?'

Like the Golden Rule, conscience is a core concept in cultures around the planet. 'A bad conscience can only make men cowardly and fearful' was how Martin Luther put it. The sixteenth-century German monk, who risked his life blowing the whistle on corruption among Catholic Church leaders, wrote:

> *Troubled consciences are like geese. When the hawks pursue them, they try to escape by flying, though they could do it better by running. On the other hand, when the wolves threaten them, they try to escape by running, though they could do it safely by flying. So when their consciences are oppressed, men run first here, then there; they try first this, then that.*

Proverbs from across cultures and across the years speak with eloquence about the power of guilt in our lives, for example:

A guilty conscience needs no accuser. (*English*)

Conscience is what tells you not to do what you have just done. (*Spanish*)

Conscience is the dog that can't bite but never stops barking. (*Unknown*)

Conscience is as good as a thousand witnesses. (*Italian*)

Clear conscience never fears midnight knocking. (*Chinese*)

A clear conscience is more valuable than money. (*Philippine*)

Conscience, man's moral medicine chest. (*Mark Twain*)

Conscience is the nest where all good is hatched. (*Welsh*)

A SIMPLE DHARMIC DILEMMA

Imagine this: a middle-manager in a subsidiary of a leading multinational energy-trading company discovers that his employer uses suspicious accounting gimmicks to cheat its customers and the public, allowing it to book enormous, unethical profits.

He is horrified that the company to which he has pledged his career would allow itself to be manipulated into such a precarious spot. He is frustrated that his co-workers are either complicit or compliant – unwilling to risk their jobs challenging an entrenched system of corruption.

Our hero has a number of time-honoured strategies to ponder:

(A) He can sit on his hands, grind his teeth, and grow bitter and grey hoping to hold on to his retirement account by outlasting the bad guys.

(B) He can dust off his résumé in the hope he can land a similar job somewhere else before he is crushed in the inevitable collapse of the house of cards.

(C) He can write a letter of complaint to the boss, and hope he escapes a reprimand, demotion, exile or firing, a very common occurrence: 95 per cent of the time, whistleblowers lose their jobs, according to the Emerson Center for Business Ethics at St Louis University.

(D) He can send an anonymous tip-off to the board of directors, or the media, or even a regulatory agency, hoping to scare the company into mending its ways, but risk being entangled or even implicated.

(E) He can seek counselling in the hope his priest, pastor, rabbi, therapist, guru or mentor will tell him what to do or how to cope with his guilty feelings.

In one way or another, in matters large and small, millions of people deal with situations like this every day. Most dilemmas are minor and we can brush them aside as inconsequential, not worth worrying about.

What happens when the stakes are high, and when two courses of action are equally compelling? What happens when dharmas conflict?

One of the surprising things we learned from the crop of gargantuan frauds in the past decade at MCI Communications, Enron and others is that some of the most loyal and committed employees were the ones trying the hardest to stop the illegal practices. Not only did they strive in vain to save the businesses from scandal and ruin, but many were ostracized or punished for stirring up trouble.

How does a person cultivate a clear conscience, and how does he or she overcome the fear of the price that may be attached to exercising it?

More about manoeuvring through these situations will be found in Part Four, 'Dharma Versus Dharma'.

PART THREE

THE DHARMA

USER'S GUIDE

Patience serves as a protection against
wrongs as clothes do against cold.

●

LEONARDO DA VINCI

THE IGNORANCE OF THE LAMBS

The human dharma – our nature – is to seek meaning in our lives and our work. Just as the essential nature of water is to seek its own level, our essential psychological drive is to seek fulfilment. It seems to be in our DNA to find that fulfilment in the comfort of being with the majority, a family, a village – among those who think, look or act like us. Hunting together on the savannah, our human predecessors discovered safety and success in numbers.

Like passion, this tendency to work together has an important place in our toolbox of motivations. Also like passion, there is a downside which the Dharma of Capitalism calls the Mode of Ignorance. In the Mode of Ignorance we follow orders or convention, even when it requires us to ignore unhealthy motivations, unethical behaviour and the knowledge of harmful outcomes.

Unlike the dangers of acting in the Mode of Passion, which are often easy to spot, the dangers of the Mode of Ignorance are often insidious because they are embedded in institutional and racial cultures. Blindly following the leader, uncritical thinking, making assumptions, moral relativism – the Mode of Ignorance is the stealthy enemy of good decision-making. It is the motivation that allows tyrants to gain power in spite of their cruelty. In our lives and work, it is the motivation that gives us permission to go along with plans or activities we know to be unwise, immoral or illegal.

Business crimes, motivated in part by the passion for wealth and material comfort, usually require ignorance in the form of rationalizing thought processes. 'Everyone else is doing it', or 'It isn't such a big deal', or 'Nobody's getting hurt'. In some cases, these rationalizations become the basis of corporate culture.

At MCI Communications in the 1990s, a junior executive responsible for collecting overdue payments from bulk long-distance telephone customers was instructed by his superiors to hide tens of millions in uncollectable receivables by accepting as payment what he knew were worthless promissory notes. The uncollectable receivables thus became booked revenue and the worthless notes went into the asset column of the company's balance sheet.

The executive, Walter H. Pavlo, knew what he was doing violated all the rules of accounting, but the orders from his superiors were unequivocal. There was a company-wide push to keep the stock price up in anticipation of a buyout in the tens of billions of dollars. Writing down receivables would have undermined the company's bottom line, created doubt and knocked down the price it could fetch.

Pavlo challenged his boss but was told, 'Every organization is screwed up. I'm not saying it's right. I'm saying don't worry about it. This isn't going to stick to you.'

Pavlo had just earned his MBA and had arrived at MCI filled with ambition and idealistic fervour. He gradually became so corrupted by the hypocrisy and callousness of what he was being paid to do that he went a step further. He allowed himself to be recruited into a freelance fraud in which he and some co-conspirators stole $6 million from the company. He convinced himself that it was excusable to steal from thieves.

When the dust had settled, MCI (and Worldcom, which later acquired it for $34.7 billion) was exposed as the largest accounting fraud in history. Not only did the scandal stick to Pavlo, he ended up pleading guilty to fraud, serving two years in federal prison, and losing the love of his life to divorce. He later told the story in his book, *Stolen Without a Gun*, a classic case study of the destructive influence of the Modes of Passion and Ignorance on a multibillion dollar enterprise.

People stuck in the Mode of Ignorance feel powerless and trapped. They become emotionally imprisoned, morally lazy or self-deluding, as innocent and oblivious as lambs. That was the case for clients of the infamous Ponzi-schemer Bernard Madoff. He, on the other hand, was deep in the Mode of Passion; his addiction to status and gratification was so intense he was willing to steal from clients to sustain the thrill.

There were investigators and sceptics who suspected that the investment returns Madoff claimed to be making for his clients were bogus. But the people who gave him their money persisted in believing he was a genius and, in the Mode of Ignorance, were easily led to financial slaughter.

One of these was a middle-aged woman who had the good instinct to get a second opinion from another investment adviser, Thomas C. Scott of Irvine, California. Scott, in a column he wrote for Forbes.com in 2009, recalled meeting her several years before the Madoff scandal broke.

> She said that she had a large sum invested with an outfit in New York (Madoff) that was earning her a steady monthly return of 1% to 1.5%. I asked her how the money was invested. She said, 'I'm not really sure, but I get statements that show trades in different stocks.'

Scott was immediately suspicious, especially when she told him that Madoff's fund was open 'only to friends and family', a phrase he knew from experience was often used by scammers to create trust. He was convinced it was a fraud and tried to find a way to ascertain the truth and warn her without causing insult or upset.

'After three minutes of listening to her wax rhapsodically about this exclusive investment', Scott wrote, 'I told her, "It sounds odd. If you could show me some of the statements, I'd like to see how your money is invested".'

Scott, who had been an investment professional for 25 years, wrote that the woman shot him a dismissive grimace:

*She clearly thought I was too dumb to grasp such
sophisticated money management. She insisted, 'He
has a sterling reputation. His clients include some of
the smartest people on Wall Street and the biggest
names in business.' She wasn't interested in anything
else I had to say, and I never heard from her again.*

The Mode of Ignorance often compels us to take up
activities and invest confidence in people even when our
inner voices tell us we may be doing something that could
be detrimental to our happiness or success. It's easier and
more comforting just to go along with the crowd.

PHARMA DHARMA:
WAGES OF IGNORANCE

One of the industries that has paid a high price for acting
in Passion and Ignorance is the pharmaceutical sector.
In recent years large drug makers have been caught using
questionable marketing tactics to persuade physicians
and hospitals to prescribe particular products. Kickbacks
and unapproved uses of medications have cost companies
like AstraZeneca enormous fines, class-action lawsuits,
and loss of credibility. In 2009, Eli Lilly agreed to pay the
US government $1.4 billion for off-label promotion of an
anti-psychotic drug.

Johnson & Johnson was once considered a model of good
corporate behaviour for its handling of a highly-publicized
1982 Tylenol poisoning incident. Someone in the Chicago

area contaminated several bottles on pharmacy shelves with cyanide. Five people died as a result, including two children in one family.

The company, acting in the Mode of Goodness, immediately recalled and destroyed $100 million in retail value of Tylenol, even though it meant losing 75 per cent of its share of the market for analgesics. But because of its rapid response and efforts to reinvent the packaging, which changed the entire industry, the reintroduction became a huge success. Within several years Tylenol had become the most popular analgesic.

In the years since it was heralded for doing the right thing, Johnson & Johnson has earned itself a black eye or two for doing the wrong thing. In January, 2010, the US Justice Department charged the company with paying tens of millions of dollars in kickbacks to nursing-home pharmacy supplier Omnicare Inc. to buy and push Johnson & Johnson drugs. In addition to allegations that it tried to hide these payments to Omnicare, Johnson & Johnson was discovered to have been underwriting Omnicare's annual national managers' meeting at a resort in Florida.

The company has also been accused by former salespeople working in its Ethicon surgical supply subsidiary of using manipulative tactics in sales to hospitals. The company periodically introduced new versions of products such as sutures and clamps that were substantially the same as the old versions, while refusing to allow the hospitals to return the perfectly good, unused older models for credit.

The tactic took advantage of the fact that surgeons always want the latest equipment, no matter how minor the improvement. A slight redesign is all it takes for a head surgeon to direct his or her hospital's purchasing agent to buy the latest model and get rid of the old one.

This squeezed both the purchasing agents and the salespeople into the same corner. The salespeople needed to sell the new version and the hospitals needed to buy it. But there was no mechanism or system for selling the old, and it made no sense to anyone to send perfectly good, expensive surgical-suite supplies to a landfill. The company's solution, according to charges by a number of the Ethicon salespeople, was to unofficially let it be known that the sales staff were free to do whatever it took to help the hospitals make the old inventory disappear.

To meet their sales quotas, the reps physically carried the old inventory out of the hospital, put it in their car boots, and in some cases hid it in their garages or sold it on the grey market to jobbers who in turn sold it into foreign markets. The hospitals never saw any money in return. It was as if all that inventory just disappeared. The practice came to light when a number of sales reps were accused of criminal wrongdoing.

Johnson & Johnson's Mode of Passion motivation, to meet earnings goals to support the company's stock price, trapped its reps between the company and its customers and effectively gave them permission to act in the Mode of Ignorance.

In every one of these instances, doing the right thing would have had a cost associated with it. Company managers would have had to find other ways to grow their businesses, which would have required an investment in research and marketing, and a learning curve. But it is hard to imagine that any lost opportunity income could exceed the cost of hiring phalanxes of lawyers, paying out fines, the damage to reputations, the disruptions to normal operations and so on. Short-term thinking creates long-term problems, like a debt that we ignore but will one day have to pay.

A company that consistently acts in Goodness should operate more efficiently, productively and profitably because it avoids becoming distracted and bogged down by controversies and legal battles.

THE PASSION OF THE CAPITALIST

During the past four decades, the standards of ethical behaviour in our financial and business practices were swept aside by the ever-increasing demand for quick profits and instant gratification. It took a global financial panic to do it, but the business community is finally coming to terms with what went wrong and searching for a way to fix what's broken.

Nobel Prize winning economist Joseph E. Stiglitz has become one of the most vocal critics of the revolution started all those years ago by another Nobel Laureate, Milton Friedman, who promoted economic Darwinism. 'We have created a society in which materialism overwhelms moral commitment, in which the rapid growth that we have achieved is not sustainable environmentally or socially, in which we do not act together to address our common needs', Stiglitz wrote in early 2010.

Business success has always required enthusiasm and single-mindedness. New ventures need a rush of creative and nervous energy, fuelled by the passion of the entrepreneur or inventor. In established companies, passion manifests itself when we rise to meet a competitive challenge or seize an opportunity, and in the quarterly ritual of meeting profit projections and the expectations of shareholders. Passion is at work when we strive to accumulate wealth and achieve status.

So the Mode of Passion has a place in our quiver of motivations. But in our ever-evolving lexicon, passion has been elevated to the status of a desired value. We are encouraged to find our passion, to 'feel passionate' about our work and our lives.

We forget, at our peril, that passion has a dark side: *Webster's Dictionary* defines it as, 'a barely controllable emotion'. In the context of the Dharma of Capitalism it describes the fleeting nature of excitement and gratification. Entrepreneurs become bored, booms turn to busts, winning loses its thrill, tastes change, relationships grow stale, the satisfaction from status fades.

Passion, it turns out, can be a kind of drug – it lifts us up and then lets us down. We crave more – victories, money, position, gratification. Like an addict, passion requires ever-increasing levels of risk to achieve the same feeling of excitement. When we don't get it we suffer, get frustrated, and retreat into ignorance or cynicism.

The ancients understood this concept well: the Latin root, passio, means suffering or enduring. Christ's Passion is the story of Jesus's persecution, not his miracles. Although the popular interpretation placed on passion has changed since those days, the basic nature of passion has not: it is transitory and unsustainable.

The Dharma of Capitalism reminds us to avoid letting the Mode of Passion dominate our decision-making. A little passion goes a long way, and a little foresight goes even further.

If you know passion is transitory, you begin to understand that the cycle of life is also the cycle of business: creation, preservation, destruction. History is littered with the wreckage of once exciting and powerful companies like Cunard Lines, Western Union Telegraph and Polaroid.

We can point to any number of companies that died and were reborn – Chrysler rose from the ashes of bankruptcy in the 1980s to once again become a leader in its industry. Some of the more enduringly successful companies have gone through the cycle from creation to destruction and back to creation again, as Apple Computer has more than once.

Coca-Cola went through a destructive phase in the 1980s when it was losing ground to Pepsi and changed the formula of its flagship drink. The new product launch was a disaster, but the reintroduction of the old product reinvigorated the company and the brand.

If you incorporate awareness of the cycle into your decision-making process, instead of fighting what is natural, you prepare for it and try to make it work for you. The most universal example of the cycle is romance and marriage. People fall in love, marry in lavish public displays with the highest expectations of happiness, and then two years later wonder where the passion went.

Many more marriages would thrive, and many bad marriages could be avoided, if the partners understood and accepted that passion has a shelf life, that contentment comes from learning how to manage the transition. Each would be more likely to ask themselves before they commit, 'Is this a lasting love or am I motivated primarily by passion, a barely controlled emotion such as fear of loneliness, physical infatuation, desire for status, and so on?'

Like many relationships, much wealth is destroyed and many careers ruined by decisions made in the Mode of Passion.

DHARMA DRAMA: AOL TIME WARNER

One of the most spectacular examples of the dangers of acting in the Mode of Passion is the decision in 2000 by

Time Warner CEO Gerald M. Levin to facilitate the media giant's purchase/merger by high-flying Internet pioneer AOL. Before the ink had dried on the deal, it began to crumble like a sand castle – a little at first and then faster and faster as the tide rolled in. The Internet honeymoon faded, the 'new' economy went into an old-style recession, AOL's growth slowed and competition heated up.

Within two years the combined companies had recorded a history-making loss of $99 billion. AOL, once valued at $165 billion, steadily shrivelled until Time Warner finally spun it off in 2009 for stock valued at less than $4 billion – two cents on the original dollar.

'Messianic zeal' was the term Levin used in a 2009 interview with CNBC to describe his state of mind at the time. He admitted to being enamoured by 'this magnificent concept' of bringing together old and new media.

In his passion to make his vision a reality, he excluded his top executives at Time Warner from the decision-making process. Except for the shareholders and professionals required to evaluate and negotiate the terms, the rest of the company's management learned the news along with the public, when they came to work one Monday morning.

Levin explained his failure to solicit input from his team as an attempt to prevent news leaks and organizational chaos. In his messianic zeal, Levin roared past all the flashing lights. Had he paused to examine his motivations in the context of the Three Modes and the Dharma of Capitalism, had he consulted some of the veterans in the company about the potential outcome of the combination, he might have recognized that it was a poor match beforehand instead of afterwards.

The AOL team had little experience with advertising sales and regarded Time Warner as an old-economy company with ossified leadership. The Time Warner team saw the young, cocky AOL executives as intemperate and the Internet as an overpriced novelty that threatened their print magazine business. At the time Levin was 61 and AOL Chairman Steve Case was 41. On every level, they came from different worlds and spoke different languages.

Had Levin stayed his hand while examining his motivations, he might have stalled long enough to dodge a bullet. The gathering implosion of the dotcom bubble in 2001 would certainly have killed off the deal and Levin might have been spared the indignity of landing on CNBC's list of the 'Worst CEOs of All Time' for masterminding 'The Worst Deal of the Century'.

Time Warner, which had once been a leading media company, is another example of what happens when the natural cycle of capitalism is exaggerated by the Mode of Passion – the level of destruction was catastrophic. No one can say for certain what might have happened had Gerald Levin and Steve Case never met. We can say that both men clearly were motivated by personal ambition and vision and that the choices they made were arrived at without regard to potential outcomes. They ignored risk in their passion for reward.

DHARMA GOODNESS:
THE PATIENCE PAYOFF

Acting in the Mode of Goodness is much harder than acting in the Modes of Passion and Ignorance. In Ignorance, anything that's not our problem is not our concern or responsibility. We avoid or rationalize away letting it weigh on our conscience. But it often does weigh on our subconscious, which can lead to guilt, bitterness, cynicism and carelessness.

To get from Ignorance through the excitement and activity of Passion and on to Goodness takes practise, thinking critically and objectively about everything we do until it becomes second nature. Acting primarily in the Mode of Goodness requires a deliberative thought process, applied to every aspect of our lives, that can start out feeling austere, even pedantic.

Corporations are led and managed by men and women who bring to their desks the influences of the modes in which they act at home. We make dozens of decisions every day in our personal lives and the mode in which we make them bleeds over into our business and professional lives. If you accept that no vice is too small to commit, aiming for the Mode of Goodness is as important off the clock as on.

An example most people have experienced in one manner or another is the checkout error in our favour. If you go to the supermarket and discover when loading your car that the checkout clerk neglected to charge for a box of cereal that was obscured on the lower rack, the first instinct may be to do the right thing and return to pay for it. But most of us will feel ambivalent.

First, in the Mode of Passion, we're busy and we don't want to take the time to go back and wait in the queue once more. It's inconvenient and annoying. We may feel foolish about walking into a store with merchandise and possibly having to explain why. Maybe we don't want to cause trouble for the clerk.

Then, in the Mode of Ignorance, we may tell ourselves that it's just a box of cereal, it's only a couple of pounds, and the loss will have no measurable impact on the financial health of a multibillion-pound retailer. We may even rationalize that it's all right to award ourselves a small discount for all the business we've given the store over the years. No one will be the wiser. It hardly seems worth fretting over.

So we get in the car and drive away with our unexpected bonus. The problem is that we also drive away with a guilty conscience, even if we've distracted ourselves from it with moral gymnastics. When we get home and unpack the shopping, the cereal box will be there to remind us that we got something for nothing, which we know to be wrong even if it was an accident.

When we sit down to breakfast the next morning, the box comes out again to remind us of our lapse. Even if we've convinced ourselves that we deserve a spot of good luck now and then, in our hearts we know that we made a decision in the car park that effectively was stealing. Something for nothing always has a price.

This example may seem trivial on a superficial level, but it is an apt metaphor for decisions we make all the time in the business of living. We 'forget' to report small amounts of income on our tax returns or justify taking deductions that are more personal than business. In professions where services are invoiced by the hour, we may pad a bit here and there to help us meet our income needs, perhaps telling ourselves that we did an especially good job and deserve it, or that we'll make it up later in unbilled hours.

In our business operations we may keep costs down by making it difficult for dissatisfied customers to request an adjustment or refund. Discount coupons and rebates that stimulate sales may be designed to be so time-consuming to submit that customers don't bother. The motivation for these two examples – choosing profit over customer satisfaction – fails the Three Modes test. Those who design these schemes are acting in the Mode of Ignorance by turning a blind eye to negative outcomes, not least of which is the tarnishing of the company's reputation, which in turn reduces its brand or equity value.

The slippery slope gets steeper: corporations manipulate earnings to keep the cost of capital down; backdate stock options to give executives windfall bonuses; allow directors to borrow the company jet to fly family members on holiday; push sub-par products because they are more profitable; cook the books to meet loan covenants; and commit cover-up crimes that are worse than the problems they are trying to conceal.

Two people who went down in flames in the first year of the new millennium discovered the staggering cost of a single moment spent in the Mode of Passion. Samuel D. Waksal, founder of cancer-drug company Imclone Systems, and his acquaintance, Martha Stewart, founder of Martha Stewart Living Omnimedia, were two phenomenally successful business people who ruined their reputations and nearly destroyed two multibillion-dollar enterprises, simply for selling a few Imclone shares just before the release of bad news.

Waksal was caught, pleaded guilty to insider trading, was driven from the business he'd founded, lost a fortune and ended up with a seven-year prison sentence. Stewart, whose thoughtless decision saved her from a temporary loss of $50,000, was forced out as CEO of the company she founded and spent five months in jail for perjury.

Had Waksal and Stewart been patient and acted on their better instincts, in the Mode of Goodness, the outcomes would have been dramatically different. Although Imclone shares did fall after the news of an adverse decision by federal regulators, within two years it had rebounded to new highs. Not only would they have lost nothing, Stewart and Waksal might have made a large profit on their shares. In 2009 the company was sold to Eli Lilly for $6.5 billion.

Waksal saved himself a quick million or two in the heat of the moment, but he traded away a king's ransom, his dignity and his freedom. Stewart, for whom the money saved was a drop in the bucket of her net worth, became the object of widespread ridicule and gossip, her brand was tarnished and lost value, and a relatively young enterprise that seemed to be doing everything right has yet to regain its footing.

The challenge in the Mode of Goodness is to accept that the benefits of doing the right thing are often unseen, difficult to identify, and impossible to measure in the same way we calculate success or failure. The impact of our choices may not be felt until years later in the forms of customer loyalty, a good reputation, avoiding lawsuits, less regulatory action and so on. Acting in the Mode of Goodness may at times feel like an act of faith in that it requires a philosophical belief in the unknowable future. We cannot predict outcomes and consequences with certainty, but we can choose to believe in the potential benefit to someone somewhere when we act in the Mode of Goodness.

DHARMA EXPOSED: A KODAK MOMENT

A perfect example is provided by an Eastman Kodak anecdote about how the company earned the respect and trust of the trade authorities in the People's Republic of China. One of Kodak's clerical employees made a minor decision in the Mode of Goodness that has become an underground legend.

The episode is retold by Ying Yeh, Kodak's North Asia Region President, in a Harvard Business School Press book entitled *Doing Business Ethically*. When Kodak first began doing business in China, before digital cameras became ubiquitous, the company shipped its film in huge bulk rolls from the United States and assembled the consumer cartridges in China.

Each master roll was subject to a substantial import tariff. Because of the company's stature and international reputation, the containers of bulk film rolls passed through Chinese customs uninspected. The tariff was calculated on the basis of the bill of lading – the honour system.

One day a container arrived with a bill of lading showing six master rolls, but when a logistics clerk opened it at the plant, he found ten. Had the clerk simply allowed the shipment to go into inventory, Kodak would have saved $1 million in import taxes.

'That was on a Friday afternoon', Ms Yeh recalled. 'The clerk immediately sealed the container, sent it straight back, and told customs that we made a mistake.

'On Monday, the clerk told his supervisor, and then we went to the accounts department with a cheque in hand (for the correct amount).' When word of what had happened got back to officials in US Customs, some of whom had been in that business for 40-odd years, the Kodak executive said, 'A lot of them were shocked; they had never heard of such a thing.

'They asked, "Did the clerk get punished because he didn't report to the manager level before he made the decision?" We said, "No, of course not. That was his job, that's what the training is all about, and he did the right thing." The follow-up question was, "Was he rewarded?" And we said, "Of course not, because he basically did what he was trained to do."'

The story spread by word-of-mouth through the entire customs system and was later featured in a Chinese Customs Service publication. 'For this, people trust us', Ms Yeh wrote. 'But credibility is a very fragile thing. It can take years to build, but it can be destroyed overnight.'

THE THREE MODES,
IN MIND AND MOTION

The way to learn how to sail a boat is to sail a boat. We can read books and take courses. We can study the dynamics, learn how to tie knots and decipher charts. We can take a weather class to be able to identify and interpret cloud formations. But real learning takes place out on the water where we develop our instincts and skills by studying how we interact with vessel, sea and wind in order to stay on course.

The same is true when it comes to adapting to the Dharma of Capitalism and striving to act in the Mode of Goodness, to stay on the course of doing the right thing. If teaching ethics in a classroom or a house of worship were enough to predict good outcomes, most of the world's problems would eventually be solved. Clearly, a leap is required between knowing the right thing to do and actually doing it. Like any skill, it requires practice and persistence. You can't intellectualize good behaviour. It has to become instinctive.

The conventional approach to creating such change in our lives and institutions is we set goals, make a plan and then execute it: we think, we study, we act and we assess the results. If we are successful, we tend to build from that. Failure is an unwanted outcome and often results in penalties for those regarded as responsible.

The dharmic process offers a second option that places less emphasis on the consequences of failure and more on what we learn from it. We can reverse the steps: we make a decision (act), we examine our true motivations and the outcomes (study), and we examine where it all fits in to the Three Modes (think). The process repeats, each act informed by and building on what we learned from the last. It's the same principle by which children learn the dangers of a hot stove. We have to make mistakes to learn how to avoid them. Permission to make mistakes is a core principle in dharmic thinking.

Former GE Capital CEO Lawrence Bossidy once captured this idea succinctly: 'We don't think ourselves into a new way of acting; we act ourselves into a new way of thinking.'

Just as the ability to navigate a sailing boat is a mix of weather, equipment and crew, our decisions are the result of an intermingling of all three modes. The dharmic decision-making process challenges us to experiment and study our mistakes and successes, to identify which mode is predominating and make adjustments to more consistently stay in the Mode of Goodness.

DHARMA MUMBO JUMBO

The first step for sceptics is to let go of cultural prejudices and defences. As you read about the ideas in these pages you may be inclined to think, 'I know all this. I just have to try harder and demand more of myself and others.'

Perhaps you find the concept of goodness insipid or idealistic. Your vocabulary may equate ignorance with lack of intelligence. You may be wondering, why can't a person be passionately good? Or perhaps what sounds like Eastern jargon strikes you as a bit mumbo jumbo.

You may in fact know all this, but you may be having trouble shaping your good intentions into a style of living and working. That's the purpose of the Three Modes toolkit, to provide a framework for evaluating your decisions until thinking in the Mode of Goodness becomes second nature.

Goodness may sound like a vague, aspirational state that is only attainable in a frenzied, complex world by checking into an ashram, monastery or spa. Goodness, however, is not a state of perfection, it is a state of mind.

Rather than the destinations or solutions we are trained to seek in life and work, dharma is an everlasting journey. It continues right to the end, as demonstrated for me by my grandfather when he spent the last hours of his life fretting about an unpaid £2 grocery bill.

The Mode of Goodness is also not a business plan, but it is a way of doing business that is purposeful, profitable and fulfilling. Rather than lofty ideals, it's about earthly reality. We feel better when we act better, and vice versa.

The Mode of Ignorance is an aspect of all people, and it says nothing about intelligence or ability. Ignorance is a term that encompasses a broad array of emotions and motivations that range from helplessness to self-delusion. We are constantly reminded that smart people are capable of spectacularly dumb choices.

As for mumbo jumbo, it may help the dubious to remember that these concepts are universal, with ancient origins. *The Bhagavad Gita*, for example, acknowledges that 'every material endeavour is covered by some fault'. There is nothing perfect in the material world, a concept expressed in the Bible and the Koran.

But you don't have to study *The Bhagavad Gita* to get the benefit of the Dharma of Capitalism. You don't even have to articulate the Three Modes to use them to evaluate your motivations and take custodianship of outcomes. The purpose of the structure is to help stimulate your awareness.

Like life's traffic signals, the Three Modes help us determine when it's safe to go, warn us when to slow down, and tell us when we should stop. This framework keeps us alert, away from mayhem, and true to our higher purpose.

PART FOUR

DHARMA

IN ACTION

Integrity without knowledge is weak and useless, and knowledge without integrity is dangerous and dreadful.

●

SAMUEL JOHNSON, ENGLISH WRITER

AND MORALIST

PURPOSE-DRIVEN DHARMA

Capitalism defines success as the honest accumulation of wealth through innovation, intelligence and hard work – profit for profit's sake. The Dharma of Capitalism challenges us to redefine it as profit with a higher purpose.

Whether you are a business leader, a professional or an hourly employee, a first step towards the Mode of Goodness would be to test your motivations and awareness of purpose against three aspirational declarations:

1 I have a higher purpose and my motivations transcend prejudice, ambition and short-term results.

2 My higher purpose is linked to the benefit of others.

3 My higher purpose includes awareness and concern for the consequences, seen or not, of everything I do.

All choices we make, from the minor to the life-altering, are opportunities to do good, to do the right thing. Most of us fritter away these opportunities by making choices carelessly, in haste, or with flawed motivations. We lurch from situation to situation, grabbing at opportunities or putting out fires rather than approaching each with a higher purpose in mind.

Dharma defines higher purpose as the potential contribution that a person can make to society using his or her skills and abilities. Higher purpose need not be grand or ambitious, and it can be fully compatible with the profit motive.

Higher purpose in the workplace can be as modest as giving good customer service or doing a job well, or it can be as broad as that of the late Mary Kay Ash, the founder of the phenomenally successful Mary Kay Cosmetics marketing firm. She defined her higher purpose and that of her company as 'giving unlimited opportunity to women'.

Higher purpose can manifest itself anywhere, even in a crucible of evil. Auschwitz death camp survivor Viktor Frankl once described how 2,500 starving prisoners chose to go without food for a day rather than turn in a single man who had stolen two pounds of potatoes. Frankl, who later became a noted psychiatrist and philosopher, recounted in his book, *Man's Search for Meaning*, a number of anecdotes to illustrate how natural it can be to do the right thing under impossible circumstances.

For some prisoners, the higher purpose was to survive in order to be able to tell the world about the atrocities committed by the Nazis. For a time, Frankl wrote, his own higher purpose was to keep alive the memory of his wife, who had been gassed the day they arrived. The higher purpose of others was to help those in worse shape than themselves.

In our modern world of relative comfort and convenience, higher purpose may seem like a vague, ill-defined ideal. In fact, many people have a higher purpose but they don't realize it, or they may have trouble articulating it. By thinking and making choices in the context of the Three Modes, a person's higher purpose will often reveal itself.

Furthermore, higher purpose – your dharma – changes over time. For a child, dharma includes being a good student. The dharma of parents includes raising healthy children and providing the necessities for their families. A teacher's dharma is to teach and a police officer's is to protect others.

Each stage of life and work brings new obligations and shifting dharma. But it is the universal dharma of all people to strive for honesty, compassion and good citizenship. When people follow their dharma, when they identify and incorporate their higher purposes into their everyday lives, they feel better about themselves, and their lives become more rewarding.

THE FOUR PILLARS OF GOODNESS

Dharma is described in the ancient scriptures as resting on four pillars:

Truthfulness
_____

Austerity
_____

Compassion
_____

Clarity

Truthfulness seems like a straightforward concept that needs no explanation. A fully dharmic definition, however, includes being honest with oneself about motivations, limitations and capabilities. This level of truthfulness is often challenging, especially when people become self-deluding.

Austerity, rather than suggesting some form of spiritual asceticism or sacrifice, is at work when we resist short-term pleasure or personal gain in favour of long-term, shared benefit. Austerity suggests patience and emotional calm. It means consciously avoiding the influence or lure of passion in decision-making and taking a mindful approach to life's problems and tasks.

It might seem austere when you are late and have to wait patiently at a stop sign, but it may well save your life. Abraham Lincoln spoke in austere terms when he described his approach to problem solving: 'If I had eight hours to chop down a tree, I'd spend six hours sharpening my axe.'

Compassion means acting in ways that benefit others without calculating or anticipating a benefit to ourselves. Compassion is at work when a top executive invests time listening to employees complain even though he has other pressing business to attend to. Compassion is when managers demonstrate that people are more important than projects. And it is at work when employers try to turn the experience of being made redundant into a chance for a fresh start.

Clarity is expressed in *The Bhagavad Gita* as cleanliness. In the context of the Dharma of Capitalism, I've chosen to use the word to describe a mind that is guilt-free and clear-eyed, allowing a person to act and think with awareness that is unclouded by a bad conscience or prejudice.

DHARMA VERSUS DHARMA

Unlike a set of commandments or laws, dharma changes according to the varied identities we assume in different areas of our lives. Inevitably, our diverse dharmas come into conflict. The dharma of being a parent sometimes conflicts with the dharma of being a CEO when work obligations overlap family time. The dharma of a CEO will sometimes conflict with one's dharma as a citizen when the profit motive is inconsistent with responsibility to the community.

Some dharmas take priority some of the time, but not always. There are occasions when the Mode of Goodness must be temporarily sidelined to deal with emergencies. The key element is motive.

An acquaintance – a European living in India – dealt with a major moral dilemma in a way that illustrates the role of context in choosing the right thing to do. This man has made it his life's work to raise money to feed and educate thousands of impoverished and orphaned Indian children. He is engrossed in his work, driven by the urgency of knowing that every day children are dying from abuse, starvation and lack of medical care.

The money to provide meals, shelter and run his schools comes from donations from business people who, in many cases, participate in and benefit from the corrupt practices so common in India. Asked how he felt about the possibility that some of the money he received was 'dirty', he told me, 'I see these kids starving every day and I don't care where the money comes from'.

A compelling argument that would stand up to his logic may seem hard to make, at least in the short term. He was far too busy saving the lives of children to try to save the world by challenging corrupt business people.

Because dharma is situational and requires taking into account both motivation and outcome, his decision initially passes the test: he did the right thing. By the same token, one who strives to always be truthful would be doing the wrong thing if he or she knew that the truth would help a murderer find his victim. No one could argue with that person for sending the criminal off in the wrong direction.

While decisions may sometimes appear to pass the 'right thing' test, there is a case to be made that continuing to accept money you know to be tainted, albeit for a good cause, validates the bad behaviour of the donor. The way around this dharmic dilemma is quite clear: cultivate donors whose money and motivations are untainted.

The man on the noble mission to rescue children may find this a challenge, but it would result in his having met the test in both the short and long term. He would also have avoided a couple of potential problems: a corrupt donor could be arrested and the funding abruptly cease; and the exposure of a corrupt donor could damage the reputation of the organization and its ability to deliver services.

Striving to be in the Mode of Goodness requires one to stop and contemplate various dharmic responsibilities to determine the broadest interpretation of motivation and potential outcome. In the mode of Ignorance, this calculation is made indifferently; in Passion, begrudgingly; and in Goodness, with pleasure and sometimes with extraordinary creativity.

Consider the dilemma once faced by a tribe of Native Americans who needed to raise money for social programmes to provide proper health care, educational opportunities, and to raise their people out of poverty. The tribe was approached by a logging company with an offer to purchase timber rights on tribal lands.

The elders had three different dharmas to consider: they needed to provide for their families in the present; to set aside resources for future generations; and to wisely manage their ecosystem. In this case, the leaders found a middle path. They convinced the loggers to harvest in narrow strips, leaving enough trees on each side of the cuts so that the canopy met overhead.

This allowed the indigenous, shade-loving understory to recover instead of dying out in the harsh sunlight that would have been left by clear-cutting. Needed funds were raised, the forest was harvested in a manner that provided for the future, and the impact on the environment was mitigated.

INVISIBLE DHARMA

A dramatic story that evolved out of the Vietnam War illustrates the concept that dharma and higher purpose are all around us whether or not we see or acknowledge them at the time. Captain J. Charles Plumb, a 1964 graduate of the US Naval Academy and a fighter pilot, had flown 74 combat missions over Vietnam when his luck ran out just five days before he was to return home. His jet was hit by a missile over North Vietnam, he bailed out, parachuted to earth and was captured. He spent the next 2,103 days in brutal prison camps before he was released and sent home.

Many years later, Plumb was sitting in a restaurant in Kansas City when he noticed an unfamiliar man two tables away staring at him. After a few awkward minutes the man stood and approached Plumb's table, pointing his finger in Plumb's face and declaring, 'You're Captain Plumb!'

Plumb was speechless. The stranger went on, 'You flew jet fighters in Vietnam. You were on the aircraft carrier *Kitty Hawk*. You were shot down. You parachuted into enemy hands and spent six years as a prisoner of war.'

'How in the world did you know all that?', Plumb asked. 'Because', the man beamed, 'I packed your parachute.' Plumb leapt to his feet and pumped his hand. The ex-sailor grinned: 'I guess it worked.'

'I must tell you I've said a lot of prayers of thanks for your nimble fingers', Plumb told him, 'but I never thought I'd have the opportunity to express my gratitude in person.'

Plumb, who has repeated this story many times in public speaking engagements, said he had trouble sleeping that night. He wondered what the sailor might have looked like in his Navy uniform – a 'Dixie cup' sailor's cap, bib and bell bottom trousers. Plumb wondered how many times he might have passed this man in the passageways aboard the *Kitty Hawk* without so much as a 'Good morning', or a 'How are you?' Plumb was a fighter pilot, a top gun, and this man was one of thousands of faceless, nameless seamen. They would have had no reason to exchange so much as a glance.

Plumb recalls wondering, 'How many hours did he spend on that long wooden table in the bowels of that ship weaving the shrouds and folding the silks of those chutes? I couldn't have cared less... until one day my parachute came along and he packed it for me.'

In his career, that sailor had inspected and packed parachutes thousands of times. It was no doubt tedious and thankless work, meticulously preparing a piece of equipment that was rarely used. He would get no medal or other benefit for doing it well. On the rare occasion that his work was put to the test, the fog of war obscured the outcome. If one of the parachutes he packed opened and a pilot was saved, the parachute got the credit, not him.

But he knew his higher purpose and felt a powerful connection to the outcome, even after so many years. Packing that parachute seemed to have become the defining moment and sustaining force in his life – his dharma.

The interconnectedness of all things is clear when life itself hangs in the balance. Less clear to most people is that the same principle applies to our work, our professions and our private lives. Doing the right thing, in the Mode of Goodness, becomes easier when you own the outcome of your decisions.

KNOW YOUR MODE

Like any skill, acting in the Mode of Goodness can become second nature, but it takes practice, discipline and the occasional short-term sacrifice. Going on the premise that we act our way into thinking (as opposed to the other way around), to figure out which mode you're in at any given moment it's helpful to keep track of your actions and outcomes and be honest in identifying your real motivations.

In the following pages you will find some specific characteristics of each of the Three Modes in different areas of life and work. Once you've obtained a sense of the behaviour that tends to define each mode, take a few minutes at the end of each day to jot down some notes about decisions you've faced or made, evaluating them in the context of the Modes, for example:

What was my true motivation?
_____

What mode was I in?
_____

Did I consider all the consequences of my actions?

In some situations you may be primarily in the Mode of Ignorance. In others you may be in Passion or Goodness. In still others the dominant mode may be unclear. Thinking about the difference will help develop a thought process for approaching future choices.

Do this for a few weeks, noting any changes in your behaviour. Give yourself permission to backslide and to be bewildered at times. If it was easy, you wouldn't be reading this book.

Worldview in the Modes

In Ignorance:

* Interest limited to immediate sphere of existence
* Disinterested in global or social issues
* Defeatist, no value seen in striving for change
* Bitter, negative, pessimistic

In Passion:

* Narcissistic
* Self-perceived as special, unique, better than others
* Living only for today

In Goodness:

* Feeling connected to the world
* Aware of a higher purpose
* Aware of consequences
* Tying personal benefit to benefit of others

State of Mind in the Modes

In Ignorance:

* Disinterested in knowledge and growth
* Lacking goals or desire to achieve
* Life feeling out of balance
* Confused, helpless, depressed, jaded, angry

In Passion:

* Highly motivated to succeed
* Mentally agitated or anxious
* Preoccupied with profit or advantage
* Desires, emotions hard to control
* Perplexed by moral dilemmas

In Goodness:

* Mind is peaceful, calm

* Sense of control over desires and thoughts

* Detachment from base instincts of mind and body

* Lacking personal agendas

* Instinctively knowing the right thing to do

Communication in the Modes

All relationships are shaped by how we communicate. Tone, word choice, timing – it all matters. Assess your current style of communicating in light of the following.

Communication in Ignorance:

* Aggressive, argumentative, defensive, profane

* Unconcerned for feelings of others

* Critical, sarcastic, ridiculing

* Cynical, suspicious

Communication in Passion:

* Rash, impulsive

* Interrupting, reactive

* Self-involved, narcissistic

* Manipulative

Communication in Goodness:

* Listening well
* Curious, desiring to learn
* Honest about motivations, feelings
* Empathic
* Inviting, non-confrontational
* Avoiding and ignoring gossip

Personal Choices in the Modes

In Ignorance:

* Seeking the easy way out
* Avoiding choices
* Disinterested in moral issues
* Unconcerned about consequences or benefits
* Unconcerned about violence or distress to others
* Prone to laziness and procrastination
* Easily discouraged by inconvenience, obstacles

In Passion:

* Motivated by prospect of reward or pleasure
* Crave personal credit or recognition
* Ignoring sound advice

* Exploiting knowledge solely for personal gain or status

In Goodness:

* Acting in a calm, regulated way
* Motivated by responsibility
* Desiring to serve a greater cause
* Sacrificing short-term gain to do the right thing

Careers in the Modes

We spend so much of our lives at work that we are inevitably affected by the prevailing energy and Mode of the workplace. If you aspire to rise above Ignorance or Passion, knowing the Mode at work, and your place in those Modes, can help you progress towards Goodness.

Careers in Ignorance:

* Poorly managed work environment
* Workers treated disrespectfully, denied choices
* Employees motivated only by a salary
* Disinterested in personal development
* Disinterested in welfare of co-workers and organization
* Work performed mechanically
* Lacking initiative
* Avoiding responsibility

Careers in Passion:

* Desiring personal accomplishment, wealth, power

* Ambitious, determined, workaholic

* Self-identifying as heroic or courageous

* Money and status trump ethics and work quality

Careers in Goodness:

* Life-long learning

* Motivated by betterment of self

* Aspiring to provide quality products or services

* Attracted to work that involves improving the lives of others

THE DHARMA OF HUMAN RESOURCES

In business settings where interests compete, it can be hard to stick to lofty-sounding principles. This is especially so when dealing with an under-performing employee, a situation many organizations are poorly prepared for and which thus receives scant attention until there is a crisis.

A manager who is overworked and trying to run a tight ship may be impatient to resolve the problem and issues a stern warning to an employee – improve or face the sack.

The boss may thoughtlessly, in the Mode of Ignorance, humiliate the person in front of co-workers.

The result of this approach is as predictable as it is common – the staff learn to fear the manager. Fear inexorably leads to resentment and diminished loyalty to the manager, the company and its values. Employees find subversive ways to express their insecurities: slacking off, ignoring problems for which they are not responsible, abusing benefits, stealing and so on.

Managing in the Mode of Ignorance invites a culture of criticism. Personnel are more likely to call attention to the faults of peers, competing to stay off the probation list. When they aren't competing with each other, employees are more likely to conspire with each other in their criticism of the boss and the company, which leads to a reputation for being a bad place to work and makes recruiting harder.

In the Mode of Passion, a manager may threaten disciplinary action, a pay cut, blocked promotion or a demotion. Looking for an excuse to fire the employee, he or she may set impossible goals. Many bosses simply dissemble, blaming pressure from higher up or some other concoction aimed at making the employee feel bad and try harder. Here, again, the results are predictable. People fabricate success, cover up mistakes, take their frustrations out on others, and sometimes turn to criminal behaviour in retribution.

Operating instead in the Mode of Goodness, managers would set an example by regularly evaluating their own productivity and performance and sharing that self-assessment with employees. Then employees would feel safe doing the same for themselves.

This transparency and honesty, with supervisory support, will help sincere employees understand their strengths and weaknesses. It will enable managers to help employees become more productive and feel more fulfilled.

The benefits of this approach cannot be underestimated. If the company runs into a bad patch, employees are more likely to remain loyal to the firm and work harder. They are also more likely to be loyal to their bosses, and more likely to defend their managers' reputations within the firm.

This open self-assessment process should be rigorous. In cases where an employee is floundering and feels out of place, it should include an honest discussion about whether he or she should be working elsewhere. A crisis like this, handled in the Mode of Goodness, can become a golden opportunity.

GETTING THE DHARMA BOOT

The responsibility many executives put at the top of their list of most-hated tasks is firing or laying off employees. It is a thankless assignment in almost any situation, especially if the person being separated is a victim of circumstance, such as a downsizing.

It's a stretch of the imagination to find a higher purpose linked to the benefit of others while taking away someone's livelihood. Human nature being what it is, we often find ourselves with conflicting emotions that can include moral superiority, power, vulnerability, guilt, depression and anger.

In the life of a business, however, firing someone can often seem inconsequential. What difference does it make how we do it, just so long as they're gone? The difference, as some mindful companies have discovered, is that doing it in the Mode of Goodness is actually profitable.

McKinsey & Company, the international management consulting firm, has seen its share of controversy over the years, but it wins high marks for its handling of separations. The firm sets the stage for leaving the day people are hired. The company tells new employees that their evaluations will depend on how good they are at 'helping and inspiring others'.

New hires also begin their McKinsey careers understanding that the company expects them to move 'up or out'. 'You constantly have to develop to be successful', the firm explains.

For those who must move out, McKinsey invests a great deal of time and expense helping them find suitable new positions elsewhere and making the transition as smooth as possible. McKinsey's reputation in this area has given it several significant advantages and opportunities. It is consistently able to recruit the best and brightest new hires because candidates know that, assuming they have honest intentions, they won't be thrown out on their ears.

As a result, McKinsey enjoys widespread goodwill among its army of ex-consultants, many of whom have ended up in leadership positions with companies that become McKinsey prospects and customers. So many McKinsey alumni have become Fortune 500 CEOs that the company has been dubbed 'the best CEO launch pad'.

This aspect of McKinsey's operation meets all three criteria in the three dharmic declarations: the company's higher purpose is to create and nurture good business leaders; its higher purpose benefits others; and it has a stake in the outcomes for ex-employees.

DHARM-ANTHROPY

The application of dharmic principles to charity may seem redundant, but philanthropy is an activity where motivations are often distorted by passion and outcomes are often corrupted by ignorance. Although giving money seems the easiest way to do the right thing, it can be one of the hardest to do in the Mode of Goodness.

Philanthropy has become so prevalent in the age of social responsibility that it is now a major industry in the United States, employing about 10 million people – nearly 7 per cent of the US workforce. The annual revenue of not-for-profit organizations – excluding religious, arts, education and human services – doubled in the decade ended in 2005 to $1.6 trillion, according to the National Center for Charitable Statistics.

The explosion in the number and income of US not-for-profits has been driven in part by tax concessions that grant special interest and advocacy groups the same advantages enjoyed by the Red Cross or a neighbourhood place of worship. The motivation for giving to a church is quite different from the motivation for giving to a not-for-profit political action group so it can produce and broadcast ads that exploit fear and prejudice. No matter how fervently each may believe they are doing the right thing, one or both may be acting in the Mode of Passion or Ignorance.

Tainted motivations are often at work when charity is explicitly offered as a transaction in exchange for a naming or branding opportunity on a hospital wing or a university dormitory. This type of philanthropy is largely inspired by ego or business self-interest, both in the Mode of Passion.

One might ask whether it matters if the cause is good. It does, in a number of very practical ways. For example, wealthy people who donate to get their names on buildings sometimes cause institutions to short-change their mission or redirect resources from more essential activities. The passion for recognition and status, to get a jolt of joy, may blind a donor to incompetent or corrupt not-for-profit management.

The flip side of these transactions is the motivation and Mode of the receiving institution. If an executive director or a board of trustees eager to leave a legacy secures a naming-opportunity donation, what will happen if, sometime later, the donor has a falling-out with the institution or becomes embroiled in a scandal? The latter has happened a number of times, especially in the past several years when many big well-known donors were exposed as frauds and their beneficiaries had to return funds, deal with negative publicity and try to repair reputations.

What happens when the donor is a business and the business falters? If this scenario seems far-fetched, consider the plight of Spelman College, the historically black liberal arts school for women in Atlanta, Georgia. Spelman received a $10 million naming-opportunity pledge in 2007 to create a Center for Global Finance and Economic Development. At the time, much was made of the benefit this would have for nurturing entrepreneurship among black women.

The donor company's name was to be prominently displayed on stationery, business cards and over the door – Lehman Brothers. A year after making the pledge, the global credit crisis had driven Lehman into bankruptcy and disgrace. As of 2010, the Center's future remained officially 'in doubt' and the name of Lehman Brothers had become synonymous with financial mismanagement and economic disaster.

In the Mode of Passion, Lehman Brothers (among other bad choices) had provided the capital to finance a major mortgage broker which, also in the Mode of Passion, was selling mortgages to people it knew were at high risk of defaulting. In the Mode of Ignorance, Lehman executives chose to overlook the possible outcome of the choices they made because the business was so profitable.

Lehman grew rich when things were going well and, in the Mode of Passion, decided to make a very public display of generosity. The Spelman administration, understandably in the Mode of Passion, was thrilled at the prospect of becoming a magnet school for black women to study global finance.

In the Mode of Ignorance, the Spelman directors assumed that Lehman's long history and good reputation meant the pledge was a guarantee. Instead they ended up with egg on their faces, having to explain to a disappointed college community how such good fortune could have so suddenly turned to ashes.

In hindsight, the Spelman directors are likely to have reassessed their deliberative process and done some second-guessing. What could we have done differently? How did this go wrong? How could we have known that Lehman Brothers was on the verge of disaster, or that the company's largesse was the result of huge profits generated by questionable practices? That's a lot to ask of the trustees of a college.

However, it is fair to ask a couple of pointed questions:

* Did a small (2,500 students), four-year liberal arts college with an existing endowment of nearly $300

million really need a $10 million centre for the study of global finance? With a graduation rate of about 70 per cent (versus 90 per cent and higher for the nation's top-rated universities), would Spelman have been better served by a donation that aimed to increase the number of students who earned diplomas? Could Spelman instead have boosted its scholarship programme?

❋ Why did Lehman, based in New York, choose Spelman, in Georgia? What was the motivation? We can't know for sure, but there were clues for all to see. The year before the donation, Lehman had been accused of discriminating against women, and a complaint had been filed accusing an executive of making a racist remark during a training session. Was the naming-opportunity donation aimed at helping young black women succeed in the business world, or was it intended to repair the firm's image?

For the sake of this example, let's assume that Lehman's donation had many strings attached: the firm's goal was to be seen making a grand gesture and the only way Spelman could get the money was to go along with calling it the Lehman Center for Global Finance and Economic Development.

Here is where the Mode of Goodness begins to feel austere, because the college trustees could, in good conscience and with good reason, have said simply, 'No thanks'. This would have been unpopular. Alumni might have called the trustees crazy to turn their noses up at $10 million.

It would have been a controversial decision but it would have saved Spelman from an even more controversial outcome and avoided a major distraction from the school's core mission.

Most of the time people give because it feels good. Social scientists who study this phenomenon report that people get an emotional lift from making a donation, and those who regularly donate or give gifts to others are happier than those who don't. But even under those circumstances, generosity benefits from the Three Modes process.

Philanthropy in the Mode of Ignorance comes with a general lack of awareness and knowledge of how the money will be used. Consequently, such charity sometimes results in harm to others and can be abused by the recipients, as it was in India when people learned to play the system of micro-finance.

Another notable example is what sometimes happens after a major natural disaster when people feel motivated to contribute money and goods. As *Time* magazine reported:

> *There is the help that is no help at all. After the 2004 tsunami, aid poured in from all over the world. But it included tons of outdated or unneeded medicines that Indonesian officials had to throw out. People sent Viagra and Santa suits, high-heeled shoes and evening gowns. A year later, after an earthquake in Pakistan, so much unusable clothing arrived that people burned it to stay warm. It may make us feel good to put*

together children's care packages with cards and teddy bears – but whose needs are we trying to meet?

In the Mode of Passion, charity is offered with pride, seeking respect and social prestige, begrudgingly, or out of embarrassment or debt. Whatever the motivation might be, personal gain is the prime consideration. This selfish type of charity gives uncertain rewards since it lacks clear thinking.

In the Mode of Goodness, charitable acts are performed for a higher purpose without concern for personal gain or recognition, with knowledge that the money will be properly spent.

When charity is in the mode of

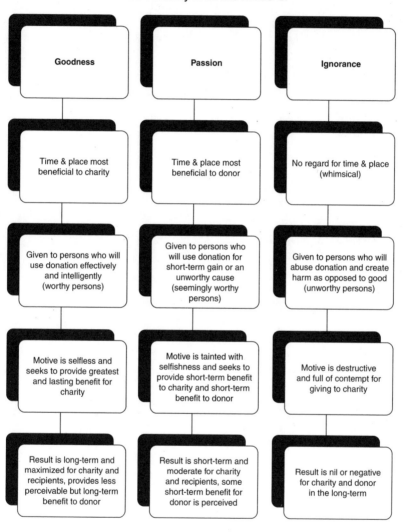

Goodness	Passion	Ignorance
Time & place most beneficial to charity	Time & place most beneficial to donor	No regard for time & place (whimsical)
Given to persons who will use donation effectively and intelligently (worthy persons)	Given to persons who will use donation for short-term gain or an unworthy cause (seemingly worthy persons)	Given to persons who will abuse donation and create harm as opposed to good (unworthy persons)
Motive is selfless and seeks to provide greatest and lasting benefit for charity	Motive is tainted with selfishness and seeks to provide short-term benefit to charity and short-term benefit to donor	Motive is destructive and full of contempt for giving to charity
Result is long-term and maximized for charity and recipients, provides less perceivable but long-term benefit to donor	Result is short-term and moderate for charity and recipients, some short-term benefit for donor is perceived	Result is nil or negative for charity and donor in the long-term

PART FIVE
THE DHARMA

OF LEADERSHIP

Let him that would move the world,

first move himself.

●

SOCRATES

THE PULL OF DHARMA

We know from experience that pulling is often more effective than pushing. It's why the horse goes in front of the cart and why motivating people works best with a carrot instead of a stick. Leaders acting in the Mode of Goodness are pulling those they lead by having a higher purpose and consistently modelling it.

The goal of the Dharma of Capitalism is to inspire leaders – whether they are CEOs, store managers or heads of households – to set examples and create environments in which the Mode of Goodness flourishes. In my research for this book, I visited a number of organizations to see what a progressive and dynamic work environment looks like and how it's led.

What I found at the heart of effective leadership was the sincere desire to benefit others. Leaders for whom this was their higher purpose had employees or group members who reciprocated with loyalty and trust. Leaders in the Mode of Goodness act with purpose and have clearly defined goals. This tends to inspire confidence and collaboration among employees or group members. This is a recipe for success in any endeavour.

Leaders in the Mode of Goodness encourage each person in their charge to set and achieve individual goals, nurture their best qualities and find satisfaction in their work. As McKinsey & Co. does, they also help employees who may be mismatched to find a better fit, turning endings into beginnings.

Those leaders find it natural and relatively easy to do all this because they apply the same ethic to their personal lives. They see the seamlessness of behaviour between work and home and thus are less likely to become embroiled in the sorts of disasters that befall people like professional golfer Tiger Woods. As the head of a sprawling empire, with responsibilities to employees and sponsors, Woods would have done well to heed the old saw, 'If you wouldn't want to read about it in the newspaper, you shouldn't do it.'

One could make the case that what happens in Tiger's house stays in Tiger's house. It's really no one else's business. But we know better, and so did he. His philandering may have been unrelated to his profession, and his transgressions may seem rather tame up against sports figures who have been involved in truly despicable activities such as sexual assault. But what a staggering price he paid for acting in the Mode of Passion.

In addition to modelling the behaviour they expect from others, leaders in Goodness make it a point to understand what inspires and drives people and teams. Giving orders is not the same as being in control, and control does not necessarily flow from higher rank and bigger salary.

The organizational chart may create the illusion that one is in charge, but as management experts point out, social interaction works like a bank account. You may make withdrawals (such as criticism or correction) only after you have made deposits (such as encouragement and praise). It's a simple concept, so much so that it's used to raise children and train dogs.

This is a good time to be a good leader. Thanks in part to the global economic crisis and generally reduced spending and expectations, workers increasingly put work that feels purposeful at the top of their list of priorities. The most intelligent and dedicated employees will give up higher salaries if it requires performing mind-numbing, routine tasks. This ought to be an important consideration in the hiring process, to identify whether a prospective employee needs money more than fulfilment. It ought to be a defining quality of a good hire.

Business leaders know better than anyone that the payoff for hiring well can be enormous and enduring. Employees with emotional and moral fortitude are more likely to feel content with their everyday work situation, more willing to work through the bumpy parts, and more tolerant of personality and cultural differences. They are less likely to drift into wishful thinking or escapism, avoid conflicts, procrastinate, humiliate others and delegate carelessly. Staff turnover slows, the cost of recruiting and training declines, productivity improves, profit margins expand.

In other words, an investment in higher purpose leads to higher return.

DELEGATING DHARMA

Managers, supervisors and executives inspired to lead by dharmic principles have the burden of inspiring others to act in the Mode of Goodness. The three declarations laid out at the beginning of Part Four serve as guidelines for changing a corporate or institutional culture.

Repeating the declarations:

1 I have a higher purpose and my motivations transcend prejudice, ambition and short-term results.

2 My higher purpose is linked to the benefit of others.

3 My higher purpose includes awareness and concern for the consequences, seen or not, of everything I do.

In inspiring others, leaders acting in Goodness seek to trigger among their employees and associates three similar ideas called realizations. You can call them by any number of names, but the meaning is the same.

Realization 1: I am more than my job, gender, ambition, religion, or political affiliation. I have a higher purpose.

Employees have a tendency to mould themselves into specific roles and rigidly identify with its function. They tend to narrow their focus to their own department's deadlines, targets and objectives, often at the expense of or oblivious to the overall vision of the company. The challenge for leaders is to create and promulgate the higher purpose or vision.

In a factory setting, for example, line workers, senior managers, and so on are all part of an ecosystem. But any one of these groups can become so enamoured of their roles that they channel all their energies and creativity into the limited range of relationships required to get their jobs done. There is a tendency to exclude other departments or stakeholders and to develop a myopic outlook in the Mode of Ignorance.

On the other hand, there is a danger in trying to concoct a sham sense of purpose with vague-sounding mission or vision statements. Large corporations spend enormous sums to come up with mission statements that convey little or nothing about higher purpose. Some prime culprits include:

'At Alcoa, our vision is to be the best company in the world.'

'Through all our products, services and relationships, we will add to life's enjoyment.' (*Anheuser-Busch*)

'Together we will build the world's most extraordinary food company.' (*Campbell Soup*)

It's hard to imagine flabbier corporate mission or vision statements than any of these. A review of a hundred corporate mission statements finds a preponderance of boastful, empty language about being the best, the foremost, the leader, the premier, the dominant, the biggest, the pre-eminent and so on. In many cases, you could shuffle the mission statements and never be able to match the statement with the company.

Happily, a few firms have managed to articulate a compelling higher purpose, for example:

> Nike's mission: 'To bring inspiration and innovation to every athlete in the world.'
>
> Progressive Insurance says its purpose is 'to reduce the human trauma and economic costs associated with automobile accidents'.
>
> Ben & Jerry's Ice Cream, started by two self-described hippies, draws directly from dharma: 'dedicated to a sustainable corporate concept of linked prosperity'.

To the degree that their executives and managers walk the walk of these mission statements and help their work forces do the same, these companies will be more likely to operate in the Mode of Goodness, be more sustainable, and be more profitable over the long run.

Meaningless mission statements are white noise compared to the recent trend of plastering the workplace with posters of beaches and mountains bearing insipid sayings like, 'The race for quality has no finish line', or 'Believe and Succeed'.

People are quick to recognize hypocrisy and exploitation, and these efforts at motivation more often than not have the opposite effect. A 2004 survey of 1,000 employees by UK recruitment firm Office Angels revealed that two out of three considered motivational statements patronizing.

A sense of purpose, whether for an individual or an organization, should be a genuine, positive aspiration that is consistent with the activities of the institution and is modelled and adhered to across the board. Mary Kay Ash, the founder of 'Pink Cadillac' Mary Kay Cosmetics, built her company by inspiring women franchisees to strike out on their own at a time when banks wouldn't even give them credit cards in their own names. It took a husband's approval and credit rating.

Every Mary Kay franchisee knew what the higher purpose was and it became the engine of the firm's phenomenal global growth, to more than $2 billion in annual sales. In that purposeful mode, the company also became an early adopter of a ban on using animals to test products.

Higher purpose can be found in any endeavour and used to inspire and energize work forces. In the banking field, for example, commercial 'relationship managers' are the salespeople responsible for prospecting for new business customers. The usual practice is to attend service club meetings (Kiwanis, Chamber of Commerce), cold calling, referrals, mailing lists, special loan rate offers and so on.

In their book, *Conversations With Prospects*, and in their consulting practice, banking experts Robert St Meyer and Jack Hubbard encourage commercial bankers to think of themselves as resources for prospects and customers. Instead of pushing products and services such as cash sweeps, credit card processing and receivable loans, bankers are encouraged to first identify companies in their markets that are compatible with the bank's culture and business model, and then provide the executives of those prospects with useful information culled from trade and business journals. In effect, the banker becomes an ally and a resource for the prospect before he or she tries to close a sale.

This approach requires managers to have patience and support the relationship managers in spending a portion of their time doing the research to get to know the businesses of their prospects and customers. The higher purpose of banking then shifts from simply meeting sales quotas or protecting turf to actually helping local companies compete more effectively and profitably. This higher purpose is to help the bank's customers thrive which will help the community thrive, and in turn benefit the bank through customer loyalty and referrals.

Realization 2: My benefit is in giving, and is linked with the benefit of others.

From the 1970s until the meltdown of 2008, the moral compass of modern capitalism has slowly swung from pure Darwinism – the market is a battlefield on which the victor justly claims the spoils – to a sometimes clumsy self-awareness of the imperative of social responsibility.

Fiduciary standards are rising, the Green movement has swept every corner of the globe, and companies are experimenting with every conceivable variation on how they operate, from big-picture issues like energy efficiency all the way down to healthy food in the staffroom vending machines.

But as a guiding principle, always taking into account the benefit of others remains difficult for many organizations to embrace and inspire among employees. This is especially true in enterprises with compensation systems tied to sales incentives, effectively pitting people against each other. But with creativity and dharmic thinking, mutual benefit can be brought to almost any shared endeavour.

For example, companies are beginning to discover the advantages of managing from the top down (pulling) instead of from the bottom up (pushing). Bank consultants St Meyer and Hubbard report that the most daunting challenge for supervisors of groups of commercial bank representatives is trying to get the lowest achieving performers to improve.

Supervisors spend little time with their self-starting, reliable top performers because, as they put it, 'I don't need to and they don't want me to'. All the time allocated for working with the sales staff is spent trying to whip the laggards into shape, a task nobody enjoys and which depends for motivation on the ultimate stick – termination.

When they reversed the process, supervisors discovered that by making life easier for the top performers (providing clerical and other back office support), the rest of the sales staff got the message that the better they did, the more help they would get. They were inspired to try harder. The top performing relationship managers were then given incentives to take time away from selling to teach their colleagues the winning techniques. Finally, the system of evaluating performance was changed from quotas and pecking order to measuring individual improvement.

Realization 3: Everything I do has consequences that will manifest in one way or another, whether seen or unseen.

Organizations tend to manage and motivate workers with tools like incentive programmes aimed at producing short-term results. This 'make your monthly/quarterly/ annual numbers' culture is a toxic moral environment in which all sorts of unhealthy behaviour sprouts and flour-ishes. The near-collapse of the global banking system was the result of pressure on companies and executives to produce large profits quickly with complete disregard for outcomes other than their own wealth and influence.

Leaders operating in the Mode of Goodness accept that it may be difficult at times to make good choices. The lost chance to enter a new global market may be the price for refusing to join your competitors in paying bribes to foreign officials. It would have been a public relations challenge for the trustees of Spelman College to refuse the $10 million donation under the terms that Lehman Brothers required, but it's a good guess that, with hindsight, they wish they had.

When you consistently think and lead in the Mode of Goodness, staying alert to the potential consequences of your choices, it becomes easier to get others to cooperate. Sacrifices are easier for people to accept and share. A leader who demonstrates that success is defined not just by output but also by input (motivation), and by outcome (consequences), is more likely to be rewarded with confidence and loyalty, which gives him or her the validation to continue in the Mode of Goodness, even when it means a short-term sacrifice.

The visionary leader goes a step further and uses his or her creativity to effect even more profound change. That's what Indian physics professor Vijay Anand did when he became frustrated enough with epidemic bribery and corruption throughout the country. For virtually any sort of official transaction, even to get a driver's licence, a bribe is expected by the clerk or other official. Doing business on the corporate level is just as dicey.

Anand came up with a deceptively simple tactic to effect big change. He printed facsimiles of Indian bank notes denominated in zero rupees, with a big '0' in the middle, and instead of 'I promise to pay the bearer', the slogan read, 'I promise to neither accept nor give a bribe'.

At first glance the notes appear to be real – they are the correct pink colour bearing the official portrait of Gandhi. Anand began giving them out in restaurants, airports and universities – more than a million bank notes in all.

This quirky crusade became a phenomenon – people began to hand them to those who were demanding bribes or acting corruptly. The effects have been electrifying. Some officials reportedly broke down in shame. The confrontations triggered conversations that had never occurred before about right and wrong and the damage done to Indian society.

His organization's website (india.5thpillar.org) explains how it works and tells some of the success stories of people who have used the zero rupee notes. Anand's higher purpose became fighting corruption. But in business, you don't have to be a crime-buster or moral leader to show others how to take responsibility for the consequences of your choices.

CORPORATE DHARMA

Businesses are beginning to move away from empty, off-the-shelf motivational rhetoric and slogans and instead making a deliberate effort to infuse their organizations with a sense of responsibility. Procter & Gamble's former President Ed Harness has said, 'It is vital that employees understand that the company is not only concerned with results, but how the results are obtained.'

This is not a new concept, but one that lost out to the Darwinists in the past few decades. As long ago as 1950, George Merck II, founder of the eponymous pharmaceutical giant, said, 'We try never to forget that medicine is for the people. It is not for profits. The profits follow, and if we have remembered that, they have never failed to appear. The better we have remembered it, the larger they have been.' Mr. Merck would presumably be scandalized by the behaviour of the pharmaceutical industry today.

In his time, Merck was applauded for his views. Many years earlier, he would have been considered a heretic, as was Henry Ford when he expressed a similar idea in 1916: 'I don't believe we should make such an awful profit. A reasonable profit is all right, but not too much. This is because it enables a larger number of people to buy and enjoy and give employment to more people.'

At the time, the *Wall Street Journal*'s editorial writers snorted that Ford was introducing 'spiritual principles in a place where they do not belong', and labelled his ideas 'economic blunders if not crimes [that would] return to plague him and the industry as well as organized society'.

History records that Ford was on the right road. His company and brand flourished by selling affordable cars that were easy to repair. Nearly a century later, the not-for-profit Ford Foundation created by his heirs remains a major philanthropic force, credited (among many other things) with having provided the seed money for the public broadcasting system's internationally successful Children's Television Workshop programme, *Sesame Street*.

Henry Ford was spared the complex forces that today's organizational leaders must navigate. It takes courage and commitment to sacrifice one's own short-term needs for the benefit of others, but the result is usually fulfilling for those who do.

This type of organizational behaviour can inspire allegiance from employees who see their managers and directors acting in the Mode of Goodness, taking into account the benefit of others. For good and for ill, employees look for cues from above, and when they perceive that they will not be exploited and will be treated fairly, the resulting inspiration can be the most powerful motivating force in the world.

DHARMA FIELD REPORT

I spoke to many business and thought leaders to learn how Ignorance, Passion and Goodness look in action.

I also studied how organizations functioned. One of the observations that came from this field research was that the Three Modes can successfully be used by three basic categories of business executives:

1 Leaders who set standards, vision and purpose;

2 Managers who support and integrate initiatives while managing the tension between short-term performances and long-term ambition, and;

3 Entrepreneurs who manage performance and delivery while building skills and resources.

The Mode of Passion, employed in a controlled manner, helps stimulate departments to achieve specific short-term targets. Passionate activities include brainstorming sessions where creative ideas are allowed to flow unfettered; setting urgent deadlines; and creating work environments that use exciting colours and modern furnishings to raise the energy level.

Where this scenario seems to go wrong is when executives and institutions attempt to turn this energized state into a permanent culture. They may expect an unsustainable level of productivity, which can lead to a tendency to recruit workers who are motivated primarily by money and will work under continuous pressure at the expense of their health and personal lives.

Organizations can do this for a time, but eventually it leads to employee burn-out, fickleness and loyalty to money instead of the higher purpose. The energy of the

Mode of Passion fluctuates and after the initial burst fades, leaders and their employees risk slipping into the Mode of Ignorance, if they fail to make the transition to the longer-term, more sustainable Mode of Goodness.

Organizations in Passion were driven by the desire for financial success with little care for the impact of their operations on the wider world. These organizations tended to be first-movers, with an intense and stimulating environment. Employees were usually over-worked. Passion was necessary to make a strong start in initial growth and early profit, but did not deliver long-term value or sustainable progress.

Organizations in Ignorance often lacked clear direction or strategy and seemed to be buffeted by market forces. Morale was low and the mood of the workplace felt lethargic and stifling, lacking a sense of higher purpose. Where low energy and exhaustion reflected the effect of played-out Passion, there was a higher incidence of substance abuse, obesity, and addiction to television and the Internet. Staff turnover tended to be higher, there was over-reliance on a small group of team members, employees were more competitive with each other, and there was little or no sense of purpose.

DHARMIC RESET

There are no quick and easy fixes. A good way to deal with this situation is to slow the pace, refocus strategy and regroup. This is often difficult for established organizations that confuse output with performance and efficiency with effectiveness. Output in Passion is high in the early stages but dwindles over time. Performance is what organizations should focus on: Input/Outcome as opposed to Input/Output.

Most organizations fluctuate between Passion and Ignorance, relying on temporary solutions, reacting to market forces, and trying to jolt exhausted or dispirited work forces out of their Ignorance. Missing is the concern for consequences and for how decisions will affect the long-term health of the business, the environment, staff and customer relations. The Mode of Passion should be used selectively, with deliberation, and as part of a programme designed to move towards the Mode of Goodness.

Organizations I considered to be operating in Goodness could clearly articulate where they were, where they were going and how their course of action had been decided. Strategies were well researched, based on facts and expertise, and understood by everyone in the organization.

One of the most striking findings was the humility of senior management and administrators who saw their purpose as serving their teams. These firms seemed to have found a balance between inspiring humility without compromising self-esteem. Standards were strictly observed but allowed for flexibility in execution, coupled with kindness towards those who had made honest mistakes.

Management saw its role as making employees feel comfortable and relaxed. As organizations moved from Passion and Ignorance to Goodness, relationships between junior and senior employees evolved from seeking or defending turf to reciprocal respect and support.

There was a conspicuous absence of politicking. Leaders spent a good deal of time in meetings simply listening to workers complaining, sometimes well beyond what most people could endure. I was puzzled about why these busy managers were being so patient, to the point of inefficiency. One executive explained that he had made a conscious decision to balance getting the work done with letting people vent their frustrations. He had discovered that just giving people the chance to be heard led to increased productivity.

In hiring, executives who operated in Goodness tended to choose sincerity over competence. As one explained it, the sincere person might make mistakes, but with guidance the mistakes could be corrected and the individual had an incentive to grow. On the other hand, someone who is competent but lacking sincerity can cause havoc below the radar.

One of the executives I interviewed had made mentoring a key element of his management process. He had become CEO of the organization after it had stagnated. The mentoring system focused on the personal development of each individual. The system grew to become the foundation of the entire organization, designed for the care and nurturing of the individual worker. That was his higher purpose and became the higher purpose of the enterprise.

Feedback, legacy planning, career development, and training were beneficial by-products. It was refreshing to see a system that went beyond superficial attempts to motivate with worn-out slogans and insincere enthusiasm. This soft approach took years to perfect but had amazing results for all the stakeholders.

At project-based firms, I noted tension between the individual worker's goals and the firm's needs. Companies in Goodness avoided the instinct to force the worker to bend to the firm's needs. Instead, this dilemma was resolved by giving the worker hope for the future by sketching a vision they could feel part of; assessing the individual's abilities and skills; and only then figuring out how those abilities and skills could be used to meet the organization's needs.

This approach is effective because workers learn that they are more important than the project, affirming self-worth and value. As these employees explore their abilities, they learn to place other values ahead of money. To make this work, the organization must truly make it possible for workers to rise up the ranks or make a smooth and successful transition out.

GOODNESS IS IN THE DETAILS

At companies that were operating in Goodness, I found a consistent and almost obsessive attention to values and that those values were the foundation of decision-making.

In one case, senior-level management became involved in a discussion about the environmental impact of the box lunches that were going to be distributed on a group excursion. They discovered that plastic materials were being used in the packaging instead of reusable metal or recyclable paper. By weighing in on such a small but visible detail, senior executives sent a clear message about the firm's values that was heard by everyone in the organization.

In some enterprises, leadership and senior management would state an opinion and then hand decision-making over to operational staff. In others where the decision was a value call, senior management would reserve the right to intervene in decision-making to ensure that organizational values were upheld. Generally, decision-making was pushed down to the lower levels and management or leadership played an orchestrating or modelling role.

Meetings often concluded with a summary statement on the importance of values. This established a consistent message that could be passed to everyone in the company without wasting time on specifics or dumbing the message down with slogans.

The feedback process at these companies was clear and unrestricted. While lines of authority in most of these organizations were unambiguous, leaders encouraged honest feedback without fear of consequences for telling the truth. Workers felt secure that leaders were sincerely interested in their opinions and interested in improvement as opposed to finding fault or shifting blame.

Individuals, including leaders, dealt with negative feedback by taking responsibility for their roles in shortcomings or disappointments. Even when discussions broached sensitive or controversial topics, the discussion was kept open and focused on finding solutions in a cooperative manner.

These organizations' approach to conflict resolution was to begin by 'changing the starting point': changing the consciousness of individuals in conflict from scepticism to a point where they could accept that the other party was not motivated by malice.

When both sides got to the same starting point, giving each other the benefit of the doubt, much of the tension and mistrust seemed to melt away and the real problem, which was usually simple miscommunication and misunderstanding, could be resolved in the Mode of Goodness.

LEADING IN STYLE

Great leaders know that when they show genuine affection and concern for their followers, they earn their respect. The leaders I considered to be the most successful were those who gave their underlings latitude to be creative and make mistakes without fear of punishment or other negative consequences. Their managers understood that their own benefit lay in the high performance of those under them, and so on down the ladder. As a result, there was less turf protecting and career sabotage.

The personal qualities of the CEO are crucial in achieving the sorts of outcomes that the Dharma of Capitalism envisions. The good CEOs are down-to-earth and accessible, yet respected. Over-familiarity is kept in check and respect is earned rather than conferred.

One employee I spoke to made a point of mentioning that in 15 years he had never heard the CEO raise his voice in anger or so much as slam a door. He had seen the boss reprimand and correct others, but always in a controlled and reserved manner.

The Goodness CEO is someone who gives of him- or herself, thinks of others, shows appreciation for the smallest successes, places people above projects, and sets goals around values and standards rather than on external achievements. Where the CEO makes it clear that the endeavour is more important than the result, people have a tendency to over achieve.

This concept was illustrated by an anecdote shared with me by a regional sales manager whose company's business depended on a global sales push just prior to Christmas. One year, during a professional development talk with the CEO, the manager said his goal was for his region to improve on the previous year's sales records.

The CEO agreed that it was a great goal, but then he added, 'Strive at the same time that your region comes in last'. It took the sales manager a while to decode what the CEO meant, but he finally realized that he was being encouraged to help everyone else do better as well.

His success was not going to be determined solely by his region's sales figures, but also by how successfully he employed his enthusiasm to inspire others. As a result, the CEO had created an ally for the whole company and, in fact, helped produce a bumper year.

At another company, a relationship manager in the hospitality division had received some valuable gifts from a client in appreciation for excellent service. The manager dutifully reported the gifts to the CEO, who instructed the manager to share them with the rest of the hospitality team to demonstrate that it was only because of their support that the manager was able to do what he did. The gesture was enthusiastically received and created a sense of shared purpose among the team members.

THE FIVE ROLES OF SUCCESSFUL CEOS

In my field research, I discerned there were five main areas in which successful CEOs tended to confine themselves:

1 Inspiration: They inspired individuals not as a motivational exercise with pep talks but as something much deeper, enabling others to develop volition and a commitment to achieve. High-profile speeches and announcements are all well and good, but real inspiration comes from example and personal conversations.

2 Values-Based Unity: They created a powerful unifying force within the organization around common values. As a result, conflicts were more easily managed and resolved because people had trust and faith in leadership. Work teams were constantly reminded about their contribution and relationship to the whole organization.

3 Relationship Management: They developed and sustained key relationships within the organization as opposed to walling themselves off or creating a competitive climate.

4 Recruiting and Training Leaders: A great deal of care went into the selection and nurturing of top people with an eye on succession planning. The leadership was directly involved in the training and education process.

5 Vision: Leaders gave lower-level managers latitude in decision-making which left the boss more time to focus on long-term strategic and value-based matters. The CEO's role was to develop those values and identify where the company was falling short. Many leaders expressed the feeling that those under them were more qualified than they and that it was their job as CEO to encourage, guide and empower those under them, and then get out of the way. They took little or no personal credit for the organization's success.

ACCIDENTAL LEADERS

The final observation about the good CEOs I met and interviewed is that most of them did not feel they were 'at the top' but rather that they, like everyone else, had their specific roles to play. They made deliberate efforts to ensure that their responsibilities were distinct from those of execution managers so they would avoid the problems that come with fuzzy boundaries.

None of the people I interviewed started out wanting a leadership position. They all got there by duty or circumstance. They invariably started off doing work nobody else wanted, often troubleshooting and then evolving into increasingly senior roles. Along the way, they sought little personal credit but often took blame.

Not having wanted to be leaders in the first place, they were fully prepared to hand their leadership role over to anyone else who was ready, willing and able to do the job. They were unattached to their positions and this proved to be a remarkably powerful tool that had a profound effect on everyone around them. It left the leaders free to make decisions based on what they felt was right without trying to manage politics or their career goals.

What I observed was an enhanced version of what is often called servant leadership. Whereas most management and leadership models are based on a pyramid structure (even if they claim to be flat), with leaders at the top and underlings below, at the companies I considered to be in the Mode of Goodness, the pyramid had been turned upside down: the leader was supporting the rest of the company.

YOU ARE HERE

In the broad spectrum of dharma, there are an infinite number of permutations of the right thing. If you've read some or most of this book, you may feel energized to take what you've learned and get busy changing your world. Before tackling the big issues, consider as a starting point the mundane decisions you make on almost any given day.

The virtue in this was illustrated for me in the dilemma faced by one of my trusted acquaintances, the CEO of a multibillion-dollar publicly held global company. We were in his London office talking about some of the issues addressed in these pages, especially about the importance of truthfulness and the challenge of knowing how transparent one can be in business without undermining your competitive position.

Always busy, he guarded his time and had trained his secretary to tell the many callers trying to reach him each day that he was out of the office, even when he wasn't. This small lie had preyed on his conscience so long and to such a degree that he asked his secretary one day, 'What do you think would happen if instead you tell callers the truth – that I'm in, but can't be disturbed?'

Together they decided to give it a try and to the degree that there were no unpleasant consequences, it was a success. His conscience was clear, and he was no longer asking a colleague to lie for him.

It was a revelation to me that a billionaire business leader with enormous responsibilities could get so hung up on a pesky, minor dilemma, and that solving it could have such a strong effect on his state of mind. He had relieved himself of an ethical problem, allowing him to move on to bigger issues with more confidence.

TAKE THE BEST, LEAVE THE REST

I've endeavoured to present the concepts of dharma in a number of ways in the hope that most people who spend time in these pages will find language and descriptions that resonate. The Three Modes, the Three Declarations, the Three Revelations, The Four Pillars of Dharma – all these constructs express the same basic concepts and guidelines for making good choices.

For those who may resist such structures, my hope is that the anecdotes and examples I've provided will be useful in creating a clear picture of what goes into a good decision and how to make more of them. If you study the mistakes and successes of others, you are already headed in the right direction.

In the end, dharma is aspirational and I encourage you to take from this material what seems most relevant in your life and career, and don't worry about getting it all down pat or being perfect. Be patient. Leave the rest for a second and third reading after you've had a chance to take some of these ideas out for a test drive. You may well find that if you re-read this material after acting your way into thinking, you will discover bits of useful wisdom you missed the first time around.

Nitesh Gor